CU00839641

Table of Contents

Chapter One – Distinguished Forebears

David Cameron is all things to all people. This is not a jibe. Launching a campaign on Britishness in 2007, he said: "My father's side of the family, by being Camerons, are predominantly Scottish. On my mother's side of the family, her mother was a Llewellyn, so Welsh. I'm a real mixture of Scottish, Welsh, and English. Her grandmother's side were Scottish Empire builders – conquered all sorts of parts of India, I think." Not only that, when Cameron visited Israel in 2014, he told the Knesset that his great-great-grandfather was Jewish. This lead Dr Yaakov Wise, a research fellow at the University of Manchester Centre for Jewish Studies, to aver that he was possibly a direct descendent of Moses.

David Cameron's great-great-grandfather Ewen Cameron left the family seat near Culloden in Inverness-shire early in the reign of Queen Victoria. After a few years with the Caledonian Bank, he joined the Bank of Hindustan, China and Japan, who sent him to their Hong Kong branch. Then when the Bank of Hindustan went into liquidation, he joined the newly formed Hong Kong and Shanghai Banking Corporation, now known as HSBC, rising to become the head of its London office. He was knighted in 1901 for his services to banking and went on to play a key role arranging loans from the Rothschild family for Japan during the Russo-Japanese War of 1904-5.

His son Ewen Allan Cameron became a senior partner in the international stockbrokers and investment bank Panmure Gordon & Co. He married Rachel Geddes, whose father, Chicago's grain king Alexander Geddes, returned to his native Scotland in the 1880s and built the mansion Blairmore House in the foothills of the Grampians.

Their son Donald also became a partner in Panmure Gordon. It was through the company that his met his future wife Enid Agnes Maud Levita. This is where the Jewish connection comes in. Her grandfather was Emile Levita, who arrived in Britain from Germany in the 1850s. In 1871, he was granted British citizenship and became a director of the Charter Bank of India, Australia and China, which became Standard Chartered Bank in 1969.

Dr Wise has traced the family's ancestral line back to Elijah Levita (1469-1549), a central figure in the "Christian Hebraist" movement, who pioneered Hebrew and Yiddish linguistic research at the time of the Tudors.

The name Levita is the Latin form of Levite, meaning a Jew descended from the tribe of Levi, the son of Jacob, and one of the original twelve tribes of Israel. According to Dr Wise, the leader of the Levites at the time of the exodus from Egypt was Moses. Modern-day Levites often carry the surname Levy, Levitan or Levita.

Having naturalized, Emile Levita adopted all the trappings of an English gentleman, owning a grouse moor in Wales and sending his four sons to Eton. One son, Cecil, became the chairman of the London County Council in 1928, while Arthur became a stockbroker with Panmure Gordon. He married Stephanie Cooper, the granddaughter of Lady Elizabeth FitzClarence, who in turn was the daughter of William IV and his mistress, the actress Dorothea Jordan. This makes David Cameron the fifth cousin of the Queen, once removed.

Steffie Cooper was well connected. Her father was royal surgeon Sir Alfred Cooper, an expert in venereal disease, while her mother was known in society for her two elopements and a divorce. Between them, Sir Alfred boasted, they had inspected the private parts of half the peers in London. Steffie's uncle was the Duke of Fife. Her aunt, his wife, was Louise, Princess Royal, eldest daughter of Edward VII. And her brother was Duff Cooper, a prominent and raffish Conservative MP who became Minister of Information in Winston Churchill's wartime cabinet. Through him, David Cameron is related to the publisher Rupert Hart-Davis, the historian John Julius Norwich, TV presenter Adam Hart-Davis, and journalist and writer Duff Hart-Davis.

There was another politician on that side of the family, General Sir James Duff, an army officer and MP for Banffshire in Scotland during the late 1700s. He was awarded £4,101, equivalent to more than £3million today, to compensate him for the 202 slaves he forfeited on the Grange Sugar Estate in Jamaica when slavery was abolished in the British colonies in 1833.

It was at Blairmore House that their daughter, Enid Cameron, née Levita, gave birth to David Cameron's father, Ian, who was born with both legs severely deformed. He underwent a series of operations in an attempt to correct them, but they remained foreshortened in comparison to the rest of his body. While special provision had to be made for him at his prep school, his mother pushed him to overcome his disabilities.

By the time Ian was ready to go to Eton, his father had left his mother and married an aristocratic Austrian divorcee who had been a family friend. They set up home in Kensington, while Ian remained with his mother in Knightsbridge. She married a younger son of Baron Manton, whose family included Baron Hesketh, the Conservative chief whip in the House of Lords from 1991 to 1993.

Despite his disability, Ian Cameron was an enthusiastic sportsman at Eton, ruing only that he could not ski. He was strong, outgoing and courageous.

Instead of going on to university, Ian trained as an accountant. He did not enjoy it and forbade his children to follow in his footsteps. Working hard he eventually followed his father and grandfather to become a partner in Panmure Gordon, though he admitted he got the position partly due to nepotism.

He moved out of his mother's house and found a flat around the corner in Basil Street, where he threw endless parties. He loved to dance and attracted society beauties.

When Donald Cameron died, he left his son over £57,000, the equivalent of £1million today. Ian then married twenty-seven-year-old former debutante Mary Mount who, if anything, came from an even more distinguished background which included a long line of Tory politicians. This began with Sir William Mount of Wasing Place, Berkshire, who was MP for Yarmouth from 1818 to 1819, then for Newport on the Isle of Wight from 1831 to 1832, before he became High Sheriff of Berkshire. His son Sir William George Mount was MP for Newbury, High Sheriff and Chairman of the Berkshire County Council. His son was Sir William Mount, 1st Baronet, and was also MP for Newbury and Chairman of Berkshire County Council. His son was Sir William Malcolm Mount, 2nd Baronet, and again became High Sheriff of Berkshire, still maintaining the family estate at Wasing Place. The 3rd Baronet was Sir William Robert Ferdinand Mount, who styles himself simply as Ferdinand Mount, a columnist for the *Sunday Times* and head of Mrs Thatcher's policy unit in 10 Downing Street, 1983-83. They had all been to Eton and Oxford.

The Mounts' entry in *Burke's Peerage* carries the name of David Cameron at the bottom and there is a cross reference to the Talbot family, which comes under the entry for the Earl of Shrewsbury and Waterford. The 22nd Earl of Shrewsbury is now the Premier Earl of England. The original title was created in 1442 for John Talbot, the heroic general who lost his life at Castillon in the final battle of the Hundred Years War. Two of his sons were killed with him, one legitimate, the other a bastard. The French honoured his courage, calling him "the English Achilles".

"In terms of English history, the Talbots are one of the great families, like the Cecils or the Churchills, only much older," said William Rees-Mogg, formerly the long-serving editor of *The Times*.

Among the family, they number bishops, archbishops, Lord Chancellors and a Prime Minister – though before the term was coined. Charles Talbot, the 12th Earl and first and only Duke of Shrewsbury – as well as being Charles II's godson – became First Minister to William III, Queen Anne and George I. It has to be said, the Talbots, the Mounts and, latterly, the Camerons are top draw.

The 2nd Baronet, Sir William Malcolm Mount, married Elizabeth Nance Llewellyn, who's second daughter, Mary Fleur Mount, married Ian Cameron. The marriage was conventional and successful. Their son David William Donald Cameron was born in London on 9 October 1966 and christened at the Mount family chapel in Wasing Place. He has an older brother, Alexander Allan, born in 1963, who went on to become a barrister and QC; and two sisters – Tania Rachel, born in 1965, and Clare Louise, born in 1971.

In 1986, the family benefited from another windfall. In the "Big Bang" – the financial deregulation of the City of London – Panmure Gordon was sold for a fortune. In 2007, it was estimated that Ian Cameron was worth at least £10million.

Chapter Two – Eton Rifles

When David Cameron was around three, the family moved from Phillimore Place in Kensington to the village of Peasemore in Berkshire. His father Ian commuted from the station at Didcot Parkway to the City of London, where he had also become a director of the estate agents John D. Wood. He was chairman of White's, the gentlemen's club in St James's, and had a passion for racehorses, owning a number of them, including one he thought might win the Derby. In 1977, he took his eleven-year-old son David to see Red Rum win the Grand National at Aintree.

David's mother Mary sat as a magistrate in Newbury and the children were brought up by Gwen Hoare, who had been in service to the Mount family for her entire adult life. She had been Mary's nanny at Wasing, then moved to Phillimore Place to look after Alexander.

The family lived in the Old Rectory. Ian Cameron was a church warden and Mary was on the flower-arranging rota. Dinner was served promptly at 7.45 pm. Impeccable manners were required. Afterwards there would be parlour games. On more formal occasions, the women-folk would withdraw while, from a young age, David would hold forth.

They had a tennis court and a swimming pool, which were open to friends. Children from the village resented not being invited. While the atmosphere at home was often bookish; outdoors the children enjoyed country pursuits. There were chickens to feed, dogs to walk and pigeons, rabbits and rooks to shoot. Later their father would take the boys shooting on Woolley Park, the country estate of the Wroughtons, another great Conservative family who provided Berkshire with High Sheriffs.

But it was tennis that was David's great passion, though he was equally competitive as a bowler and a batsman, especially at the annual cricket match held between teams raised by him and his brother, which was played at either Peasemore or Wasing.

David and Alexander shared a room until they went to prep school at the age of seven. Though they teased each other, they were eager to please. Their parents rarely had to raise their voice to them. School reports were read out formally by their father before the boys had a chance to see them. If they had fallen below standards, his father would merely say, in reproof: "I see."

Once, when David had got into a scrape at Eton, his father simply told him that he did not pay the massive school fees for him to break the rules.

Neighbour and school friend Pete Czernin said: "His parents were fantastic. They were never pushy with their children; they gave them all implicit confidence without cockiness."

"Dave inherited his father's cheek and energy and his mother's common sense – he's very uncomplicated," said cousin Ferdinand Mount. "He was the kind of boy who did his homework and then had a good time with his friends.''

Cameron particularly looked up to his father.

"I never thought of my father as disabled. He was always so optimistic," he said. "He is my role model. Dad has never let his disability hold him back. He has proved that you can do anything you want in life. He was an amazingly brave man. I think I got my sense of optimism from him."

And he was uncomplaining.

"Whingeing wasn't on the menu," one family member told the *Guardian* and a friend talked of the "subconscious drive that Dave has got from Ian's incredible example. Ian has vast enthusiasm – which Dave inherited and a sort of unstoppableness."

Cameron particularly remembered his father's diligence.

"My father used to work really long days but he always had time for the parochial church council and the parish council," he said.

Before the 2010 election, he also thanked his mum and dad for their values.

At the age of seven, David Cameron followed older brother Alex to Heatherdown Preparatory School at Winkfield, near Ascot. The school boasted among its alumni Prince Andrew and Prince Edward. The Queen would sometimes appear in a green station-wagon to drop off her sons. Once she turned up at the school play to see the young David Cameron dressed as a rabbit.

For the first term, the new boys were kept in an annex called Heatherlea, where they were cosseted and allowed pillow fights. Once they were accustomed to being away from home, they were put on a stricter regime, sleeping in a dormitory of twelve where the only comforts allowed were their own teddy and a rug brought from home to cover the wooden floorboards.

Religion framed the day. There were prayers before breakfast and service in the chapel before supper. All the masters came from public schools and the teaching methods were old fashioned. The books of the Bible, Latin declensions, and the dates of the kings and queens of England were learnt by rote.

A tubby child, Cameron said he "lost a stone every term because the helpings were so small". Otherwise, a teacher said he was "a natural boarding-school boy … easy to get on with … just a middle-class boy from a nice family".

Heatherdown was also unrepentantly posh. At sports day, there were three loos – Ladies, Gentlemen and Chauffeurs.

"It was deadly serious," said former teacher Rhidian Llewellyn. "The drivers were not supposed to mix with the other guests."

One can only supposed that the pilots of the two or three helicopters that flew some of the parents in were also allowed to use the Chauffeurs' loo.

Along with the Queen, the parents of the "toffs", as Llewellyn called them, included two Princesses, two Marchionesses, one Viscount, one Earl, one Lord, four Sirs, eight Honourables, one Commodore, one Brigadier, one Major and two Captains. One pupil, the son of an MP, said with slight exaggeration that he was one of the few boys who did not change their name during their time there due to some inherited title.

One of the virtues inculcated into the boys was *noblesse oblige*. Another was good manners. When he felt that the standards were slipping, the headmaster sent the boys out on the rugby pitch to doff their caps to the corner flags. Otherwise discipline was administered with a clothes brush to the seat of the trousers. David Cameron suffered this punishment after stealing strawberries from the kitchen garden.

Among Cameron's closest friends was Peter Getty, grandson of the oil tycoon John Paul Getty. In 1978, to celebrate Getty's twelfth birthday, Cameron and three other boys, with Llewellyn as chaperone, flew on Concorde to Washington DC, courtesy of Getty, with the eleven-year-old David swigging free glasses of Dom Pérignon '69. After driving around DC in an air-conditioned Lincoln Convertible, they went sight-seeing in New York, before flying on to Disney World and the Kennedy Space Centre in Florida, Las Vegas, the Grand Canyon, Hollywood and Getty's home in Pacific Heights in San Francisco.

That year, according to his school report, Cameron was ranked last in the sixth form, following poor results in Latin, maths, geography and French. However, his former headmaster James Edwards leapt to his defence, saying he was no "dunce", rather the opposite, as he had been promoted into the sixth form at the age of eleven. Dissenting, Llewellyn said that Edwards picked "the stable rather than the colt". If a boy came from the right background, he was selected. Heatherdown's job was to prepare boys for Eton. In the summer of 1979, Cameron passed his Common Entrance exam and was accepted.

At Eton, Cameron at last had a room of his own and got used to wearing a tailcoat. He also had the protection of his older brother, who was a popular boy three years above him. But this meant he also had to live in his shadow. While Alex excelled academically, Cameron minor's performance was considered mediocre. He was not at the bottom of the class, nor was he at the top. His maths teacher did not even remember him, though he recalled all the other boys who went on to be famous.

The same lapse afflicted David Guilford, who remembered teaching Classics to Boris Johnson. Guilford said: "I also taught David Cameron, but I don't remember him at all – he must just have done what he was told."

Others remember that Cameron could hold his own and showed an interest in literature, music and art – thought not politics. He had no grounding in it.

"Although I'm sure my parents voted Conservative," he said, "it wasn't an especially political household."

He was kind to other boys and made friends at school that he would keep for the rest of his life. But outside school, he was said to be "a typical Etonian, rather full of himself". A contemporary, Marcus Warren, said: "Cameron was posh, even by the standards of Eton."

Although Cameron said he "wasn't a complete rebel", he did enjoy a sly cigarette and a swig of wine or beer behind the cricket pavilion.

At thirteen, journalist Caroline Graham says he was an "expert kisser". He admitted to having a poster of the American model Cheryl Tiegs in a pink bikini and, sheepishly, the bare-bottomed Athena tennis girl on his wall. Otherwise his interests were art and sport.

He claimed that The Jam's "Eton Rifles" was one of his favourite songs and he was in the cadet corps, the target of the track. He also learnt the drum break from Phil Collins' "In the Air Tonight", which is also thought to be a favourite of Ed Miliband. Cameron used a UB40 track as the accompaniment to a presentation he did on poverty and unemployment. He then announced that he wished to be called "Dave". It was cooler.

At sixteen, he already had a girlfriend, Lydia Craig, now Lydia Dickinson, the daughter of a fine-art auctioneer who was a good friend of his father. The couple had joined blonde Lucy Wigram – now Lucy Sangster – the daughter of property developer Anthony Wigram and her date at the 1983 Freedom Ball at the Café Royal near Piccadilly. They danced to the outrageous ska band Bad Manners and raised £7,000 for Amnesty International. Lydia went on to be a designer on *Penthouse* magazine.

She was the first of many. "Dave never had any trouble pulling," said one of his friends. He liked aristocratic girls with an artistic side to them and went out with "some real crackers".

Six weeks before taking his O-Levels, Cameron was caught smoking cannabis. He admitted the offence and had not been involved in selling drugs, so he was not expelled, but was fined, confined to school grounds, barred from Open Day and given a "Georgic". This was a punishment that involved copying out five hundred lines of Latin text. He took his punishment manfully and did not split on the others involved.

He has described his twelve O-levels as "not very good", but he got three As at A-level, in history, history of art and economics with politics. It was only then that he "got going academically," he said. One teacher described him as a late developer.

In history, he specialized in the Spanish Civil War. His topic in art history was Augustus Pugin, but not for his work on the Palace of Westminster, but that at Chirk Castle in Wales, as he had private access through a relative. In 1983 he won the Trials Prize for Politics, then went on to study the Troubles in Northern Ireland. But his biggest mention in the Eton school magazine was when he sprained his ankle dancing to bagpipes on a school trip to Rome. He explained that they were busking on the Spanish Steps to raise money for booze.

Outside his schoolwork, Cameron did not get involved in politics at Eton, even during the furore that gripped the school when the school magazine published an article by James Wood attacking Thatcherism. But the seeds had been sown. John Clarke, who taught Cameron politics as he prepared for Oxford, said: "I'm pretty sure I viewed him as politically ambitious even then. He was articulate and politically motivated and interested. He was interested in the business of politics, in politics as a profession, even at that stage. I don't think he'd planned it out in the way Heseltine is supposed to have done. He found politics stimulating, in a good pragmatic Conservative way."

Friends said he already had ambitions to be Prime Minister. But Cameron denied making Michael Heseltine-like career plans that would take him step by step to the top office.

"Even at university I didn't know what I was going to do next," he said.

Besides, becoming Prime Minister then seemed out of the question in the meritocratic eighties. One of his friends at Eton remembered walking with Cameron between lessons and looking up at the statues of past Etonian Prime Ministers.

"We were convinced there would never be an Etonian Prime Minister again," he said. "I certainly didn't think Dave would have a go at it. His only acting roles at school were as a serving-man and as a girl. He was never outrageously extrovert – just quietly popular."

Still, there were stirrings. He bristled against the "Common Market" and wrote a thoughtful review of a talk by former Labour industry minister Eric Heffer. In his formative years, he took his inspiration from far and wide.

"One of the books that got me interested in politics was Tony Benn's *Arguments for Democracy*, which is just a great book," he said. "Lots of it I disagree with, but I loved reading it. I like being stimulated by things I disagree with, almost rather than reading something and saying: 'Yes, that is my creed.'"

Though he attended Eton's Political Society – whose guest speakers during his time included Lord Home, Lord Carrington,

Frank Field, William Waldegrave, Grey Gowrie and Len Murray – he was not on the committee like Boris Johnson, so he did not get a chance to talk with the speakers or dine with them afterwards. But then he had connections of his own, and went to Downing Street to interview Ferdinand Mount for the school magazine.

School chums talked of his assuredness – which some would dismiss as arrogance. Others said that he embodied the Etonian sense of entitlement, in contrast to other alumni who felt uneasy at the idea of privilege. He was not, however, a member of Pop – Eton's self-elected elite. He did become captain of his house though.

With politics now his forte, his tutors advised studying philosophy, politics and economics at Brasenose College, Oxford. He sat the entrance exam at the end of the Michaelmas Term, after sitting his A levels the term before. This so-called "seventh term" entrance has since been banned as it gave too much of an advantage to the public schools. At his interview, he was caught out bluffing about how much philosophy he had read, but was accepted anyway.

Before going up to Oxford to study Philosophy, Politics and Economics he took a gap year, working initially for his godfather, Sussex MP Tim Rathbone, who he described as "a nice guy but a bit of a wet". Rathbone was expelled from the Conservative Party for supporting the pro-European Conservatives in the 1999 Euro-elections. As an intern, Cameron would watch debates in the House of Commons from the public gallery and witnessed Enoch Powell in action.

After three months, Cameron went to work as a shipping agent for Jardine Matheson in Hong Kong, a job he had secured through a friend of his father. Company accommodation was provided and he got a taste of expatriate life. Three months later, he moved on to Japan, then headed homewards on the Trans-Siberian Railway.

While taking a short break at a Black Sea resort on the way, he claimed that an attempt was made to recruit him and a school friend as KGB agents. It would be interesting to think of David Cameron as the Kim Philby *de nos jours*.

Chapter Three – Buller Boy

David Cameron went up to Oxford in 1985 to read PPE at Brasenose College, which had resisted pressure to take in more students from state schools. Though he worked hard, he also relished his spare time. With his sister, he took Mick Jagger's daughter Jade punting. The next day Jagger phoned Cameron's mother demanding: "What's all this my daughter has been getting up to with your son?"

Apparently Mick had misheard the word "punting" and mistaken it for "hunting" – despite having sympathy for the devil, he disapproved of blood sports.

Cameron also hung out at Hi-Lo café with its Rastafarian owner Hugh "Andy" Anderson.

"David was very interested in his music," said the Jamaican, who had come to the UK in the 1960s. "We talked about reggae, blues, jazz all sorts of things. He was one of our regulars in the mid to late eighties and, like a lot of people, I think he kept coming back because he liked the atmosphere."

When Andy had to serve a drink to a customer, he would hand his one-year-old son to David, who would bounce the child on his knee in front of the television. Like many a student addict of daytime television, he never missed *Going for Gold* with Henry Kelly.

"David never mentioned anything about his interest in politics," said Andy. "I only found out about his interest from one of his friends."

According to fellow student Steve Rathbone, Cameron avoided student politics because "he wanted to have a good time". Amidst the political turmoil of the time, there was no doubt that he was a rabid Thatcherite though.

Nevertheless Rathbone – a state-educated "Stain", in Eton parlance – said: "He was clearly an Etonian, but he wasn't swaggering around in a braying, Sloaney way. Equally, he wasn't trying to be something he wasn't. He never tried to adopt an estuary accent, as many students do from major public schools, or wear right-on trendy clothes. He was a good mate of people from very different backgrounds."

Polite and hardworking, it was clear that Cameron was out to get a First, spouting Locke and Hume confidently in seminars. However, he did not take the easy option of dropping one of his subjects and taking an extra paper in the other two.

"He partied too," said James Fergusson, a chum from school, "but he was incredibly organized about it."

That included donning a tailcoat for smart dinner parties, though he won plaudits from other quarters when he persuaded Dr Feelgood to play at the college's May Ball. And, of course, he was a member of the Bullingdon Club.

Thought to have been founded in 1780 as an all-male sporting club, its membership was limited to thirty, by invitation only. Over the years it had become a dining and drinking club. Members dressed for their annual Club dinner in hand-tailored navy blue tailcoats with a velvet collar, offset with ivory silk lapels, brass monogrammed buttons, a mustard waistcoat, and a sky blue bow tie. Only old Etonians need apply. David Cameron, George Osborne and Boris Johnson were all members. Bullers drunken antics were legendary. During the Thatcher years, it was said, they were at their snobbish and self-regarding worst.

"If you weren't socially interesting, one of the in-crowd, he would be very dismissive," a contemporary said.

Part of the initiation was to have your room ransacked. When Cameron returned to find the place trashed, he reported it to the Dean, who then wanted to know the names of the culprits. The Bullers had a code of silence, so he had to bear the penalty alone.

Though it was natural for Cameron to join such an elite institution, he avoided its excesses. No one ever saw him uncontrollably drunk.

"Dave is a cautious man," said another friend, "someone who would think twice before throwing a bottle at a policeman."

The joke was that Cameron went along to Bullingdon dinners for the conversation – "a bit like the man who buys *Playboy* magazine for the interviews," said Cameron's biographers Francis Elliott and James Hanning. On the famous night when a plant pot was thrown through a restaurant window, the police were called and Boris Johnson put on a surprising turn of speed. Cameron retired early and was at home tucked up in bed.

Cameron was also a member of another dining club called the Octagon. Their uniform was a brown tailcoat with yellow lapels and a yellow bow-tie.

According to the club's records, on 19 February 1987, members "met for dinner in Mr Cameron's rooms in celebration of the St Valentine's day's massacre". Alongside a list of female guests was written "You sexy things" and "There have never been sexier waitresses; methinks my mind doth split at the thought".

Close to Mr Cameron's signature was the name Fran Ferguson, who was his long-term university girlfriend – though in his first term, he dated Catherine Snow, niece of banker Charles Hambro and stepdaughter of Viscount Hampden. Another flame was Alice Rayman, who went on to marry the son of former Tory Cabinet Minister Lord King.

Another night, an Octagon dinner was held at the Luna Caprese, an Italian restaurant in north Oxford.

"Preprandial drinks were taken in Mr Cameron's rooms", the record said, then the members embarked on a seven-course meal, including turtle and sherry soup. There was a five-course wine list, beginning with Corvo Duca di Salaparuta, passing through Marguerite Christel Champagne and ending with the club's stable tipple, Graham's 1977 port.

In a rare political act, he had a party in his room in June 1987 to celebrate Margaret Thatcher's third election victory. Otherwise, he left the politics of the Oxford Union and the University Conservative Association to the likes of Boris Johnson, Michael Gove and the other rising stars of the Tory Party. He only attended the Union if there was an interesting speaker. He supported the decision to let Gerry Adams speak there, though regretted it afterwards.

After eighteen months, Cameron bowed out of the Octagon. He took a temporary job shifting crates to earn enough money to take a holiday with Fran at her parent's place in Kenya. To impress her parents he brought a gift with him. It was a Monty Python record that included a sketch joking about Hitler. Fran's mother was German. Nevertheless she was sufficiently impressed to tell Fran "that chap is going to be Prime Minister one day".

As for Cameron, he had such a good time he missed his plane home and had to stay another week.

Though they enjoyed each other's company, David and Fran split up after eighteen months as she took up too much of this time when he wanted to study.

"I wanted to have arguments and be distracted, but when someone is very ambitious and wants to get a First, they don't want someone demanding too much of them," she said. "I was also quite jealous and would provoke him to try to shake him out of his self-assuredness."

Fran was so upset when the affair ended she tried to get a friend to intercede for her. Cameron was unbending, though he still wanted her to like him.

Others girls were picked up at sherry parties or in the Playpen nightclub. Women, it seemed, were attracted to his sweet nature – he cried openly at the end of a play or film.

Seizing another chance to travel, he renewed his acquaintanceship with America on a five-week sojourn at California's Stanford University, where he wowed fellow students with his unwitting impersonation of Hugh Grant.

After two years living in college, Cameron moved into private accommodation with some friends. Sometimes he would cook – pheasant was his signature dish. Otherwise there was a kebab shop close by, or the Hi-Lo where he would eat jerk chicken and goat curry, washed down with Red Stripe or overproof rum. There was plenty of booze back at the house too.

One of his housemates, Giles Andreae, who was also a family friend, was diagnosed with cancer and underwent a debilitating course of chemotherapy. Cameron drove him down to Peasemore in his battered Volvo and tended him there. He even took time off during his finals to look in on his friend.

While Cameron shied away from university politics, he could not avoid the current debates which were plainly part of his course. One of his tutors was Vernon Bogdanor, an informal advisor to the Social and Liberal Democrats, which morphed into the Liberal Democrats in 1989. This did nothing to shake Cameron's position as a pragmatic centrist Conservative. As a result, he lost little sleep over the broader philosophical questions he confronted in his philosophy course. Nevertheless, he put in the work to get a First. He conceded later that it was naff to be proud of your degree, but he was proud.

Chapter Four – The World of Westminster

It may seem odd that a man who showed little interest in frontline politics at university should storm Westminster as soon as he left. In fact, David Cameron had applied for a number of jobs in the City and journalism before his finals, and been turned down. But some "judicious prodding" from Buckingham Palace landed him a job at Conservative Central Office.

Robin Harris, the director of the research department there, said: "He applied to the research department, but there were no spaces. Then we received a call from a royal equerry wanting to know why he had not been hired."

When the story came out, Cameron admitted that strings were pulled on his behalf by some at the Palace.

"I had a godmother whose husband worked there, who knew Robin or something," he said. "Anyway, I hope he doesn't regret employing me."

Cameron's godmother was Fiona Aird, whose husband Captain Sir Alastair Aird was variously comptroller and equerry to the Queen Mother. Others have suggested that the puppet master was neighbour and family friend Sir Brian McGath, private secretary to Prince Philip, though he was a referee for the job. Both denied making the call. Nevertheless, it can't hurt to have friends in high places, though other candidates were understandably disgruntled.

He started work in Smith Square in September 1988. The Conservative research department is the fast-track to high political office, as other alumni will attest. Then it was full of right-wing zealots who called Mrs Thatcher "mother". Cameron was handed the Trade and Industry, Energy and Privatization portfolio. He worked hard, shone and his natural sociability won him friends, many of whom proved useful when his political career took off. Among them were fellow Old Etonian Ed Llewellyn who became his Downing Street Chief of Staff and Ed Vaizey, son of Lord Vaizey and a something of a star at Oxford, who became Minister of Culture. Other inmates were equally well connected.

Catherine Fall became his Deputy Chief of Staff. Steve Hilton, who he used to take holidays with, became his director of strategy. And Peter Campbell became a special advisor who helped Cameron prepare for Prime Minister's Questions.

Outside the inner circle of high-fliers, Cameron's brisk manner was sometimes considered bumptious, if not bullying – a man who liked to make himself look good at the expense of others appearing stupid, it was said. Not for him boozy lunches or a glass of wine in the office. He worked long hours and was clearly fiercely ambitious. He was also known for his good manner and all the girls in Conservative HQ fancied him. In 1990, he started an office romance with Laura Adshead, daughter of a prominent diplomatic family. When he broke it off, she had to take compassionate leave to recover. Later, Laura had problems with alcohol and drugs. There was speculation that this was fall-out from the affair. Eventually she became a nun.

Another girlfriend who was upset when they parted was Lisa de Savary, daughter of property developer Peter de Savary. She fell for him in a big way, according to a friend, but "Dave kind of dumped her and she was very cross. It all left rather a nasty taste."

The break-up did not put Lisa off politics. She managed her father's campaign as a parliamentary candidate for James Goldsmith's Referendum Party, and later married a banker and went to live in Bahrain.

The research department again offered a chance to travel. Within a few months of starting, he took an all-expenses-paid trip to apartheid South Africa. The trip was laid on by lobbyists Strategy Network International, later embroiled in the cash-for-questions scandal. Civil servants were told to shun these lavish jollies but, to the members of the Conservative research department, they were considered a perk. Cameron's travelling companion on this trip was a gay, black, master of foxhounds Derek Laud, who went on to become a contestant on *Big Brother*.

The job was not terribly well paid and Cameron shared a flat in South Kensington with his old friend Pete Czernin, whose wealthy family could trace its roots back to Tudor times. Interviewed in 2005, Czernin, then a film producer, apologized that he had not dirt to dish.

"You're never going to get Dave in a 'Six-in-a-Bed Supermodel Drug Orgy'," he said. "Sorry, that's just not Dave."

31

Indeed, Cameron now refused a joint when offered it; his eyes were firmly set on a political career. He was more interested in debating over the dinner table. Friends said that it was there that he learnt all the tricks – playing to the gallery, puncturing a counter argument with a quip, changing the subject, overwhelming the enemy with facts and figures. He was always out to win the argument, whatever the cost.

The director of the research department's political section, Guy Black, spotted Cameron's killer instinct to spot and exploit an opponent's weakness and poached him. And when Black moved on, Cameron stepped in as his replacement.

Although she had won three elections, Mrs Thatcher was becoming increasingly unpopular over the poll tax. As head of the political section, Cameron attended a secret strategy meeting at Hever Castle in Kent. This put him in with Andrew Lansley, the new head of the research department.

Lansley had decided the department's strategy. Now they were act as if the Conservatives were in opposition, taking every opportunity to attack Labour leader Neil Kinnock to distract attention from the government's problems. In charge of this negative campaigning was David Cameron who was to brief Cabinet ministers on what line to take in media appearances.

When Nigel Lawson resigned as Chancellor, Cameron accurately spotted that Mrs Thatcher's days were numbered. Subtly, he swung behind Michael Heseltine, now seen as the coming man.

Nevertheless, when Mrs Thatcher finally resigned, he said he was "very sad", though he had only met her twice.

"The first should have ended my political career before it even began," he said when a new MP. "I was the trade researcher at Central Office and she asked me what the trade deficit was. I didn't know.

"The second was at her birthday lunch a couple of years ago. She commiserated that Labour had stolen Tory language, which she acknowledged made fighting them more difficult. Fixing me with her famous stare, she said there was one thing they would never understand – the importance of 'liberty under the rule of law'."

With John Major rather than Heseltine replacing Mrs Thatcher as PM, Cameron was eager to make a good impression. Over eager, perhaps. Attending a debate in the House of Commons, he inadvertently sat in a box reserved for civil servants, inviting a rebuke from the Speaker that earned him his first mention in the national newspapers.

Under the new regime, Cameron's first job was to write a guide to the campaign should Major decide to go to the country, working closely with Saatchi & Saatchi. He was then called into Downing Street to help Major prepare for PMQs, while new MP David Davis became, effectively, his goffer, running friendly questions to loyal backbenchers.

On 30 June 1991, the Atticus column on the *Sunday Times* mentioned that Cameron was responsible for Major's performance which had "become sharper of late". He had "Neil Kinnock squirming on Thursday when he brandished a dreadful piece of doublespeak from Tony Blair, Labour's employment spokesman". The killer phrase was "those words would make a weasel blush". Two months later, *The Times* said that Cameron was "being tipped as the man to watch".

But then, of course, from his contacts at Eton and Oxford, he has lots of friends in the press. The story was that the twenty-five-year-old Cameron was to replace Judith Chaplin as the Prime Minister's political secretary. In the end, the job went to Jonathan Hill, an older and more experienced pair of hands.

Instead Cameron was to brief John Major and Conservative Party Chairman Chris Patten for their daily press conferences in the run-up to the 1992 general election. It was, he said, a "pretty hairy job". Working up to twenty hours a day, he was one of the "brat pack" of young party strategists who slept in the "bunker", the headquarters of the campaign in a rented house in Gayfere Street, a stone's through from Central Office. The job had its dangers.

"I vividly remember being pinned to the wall and screamed at by Alastair Campbell, then political editor of the *Daily Mirror*, after the Conservatives' afternoon press conference," said Cameron. "I'm still waiting for my campaign medal from John Major."

He got into another fight with a member of his own party, Energy Secretary John Wakeham, for tinkering with quotes in a press release. Cameron was accused of being "at best cavalier... at worst contemptuous of the truth".

Cross words were also exchanged with John Major and, strangely, Cameron's name does not even appear in the index to John Major's autobiography. This is all the more peculiar when you consider that Cameron briefed him for PMQs twice a week for a year.

In the end, starting work each day at 4.45 in the morning proved too much for Cameron. Having been passed over for the job of political secretary, he said he had decided to quit politics and pursue a career in journalism.

To Cameron's surprise, the Conservatives won the 1992 election. Nevertheless, the brat pack seized the opportunity to break out the champagne. They then trooped across the Smith Square to the Labour headquarters, Transport House, to jeer at the losers, before continuing the revelry at Maurice Saatchi's house.

The following day, there was more triumphalism from "Chris Patten's babes". *The Times* reported: "Having been universally blamed for the Tories' lacklustre campaign, they felt vindicated as they opened yet another bottle of champagne at Conservative party headquarters. David Cameron , aged 25, an Old Etonian, said: 'The brat pack hits back.' Mr Cameron, who briefed John Major and the party chairman twice a day, said: 'Whatever people say about us, we got the campaign right.'"

But along the way Cameron had damaged his standing in the party.

Tory grandee Lord McAlpine wrote: "I do not know Mr Cameron and from what I hear of him I have no desire to. It is tempting to put these appalling creatures out of one's mind."

The former Tory party treasurer went on to remark on his "obvious arrogance", adding: "If Cameron were a dentist, I'm not sure I'd let him touch my teeth."

Nevertheless, Cameron could not help congratulating himself. In his campaign headquarters, he had a scorecard that read: "Played one, won one."

Despite his vow to quit politics, Cameron was hooked. He was given a job as special advisor to the Chancellor of the Exchequer Norman Lamont, who considered him too young. But with Britain's economic woes, Lamont had not been having a happy time in Number Eleven. Things got worse when it came out that he had inadvertently let his Notting Hill flat to sex therapist Lindi St Clair, aka Miss Whiplash. He badly needed a PR make-over and Number Ten decided that Cameron was just the man to do it.

His new colleagues, including Lamont's Chief Secretary Michael Portillo, were impressed. But Portillo added a caveat: "I have heard he is not, sometimes, as nice in private as you might think."

With the election behind him, Cameron took time to relax at Oxfordshire shooting parties. He was seen smoking a cigar and sporting red braces, popular with Big Bang bankers at the time. He took up playing bridge, running a school in the £130,000 flat he bought in Notting Hill. He also obtained a battered white BMW, which he drove to work.

With the affair with Laura Adshead behind him, he was now a free agent and journalist Petronella Wyatt, daughter of ex-MP and political columnist Woodrow Wyatt, went weak at the knees over him. They met at a party at Number Eleven.

"He had me in his arms. His breath was warm on my face. Oh, be still my beating heart! It all lasted less than an hour, but I shall never forget," she said.

Some thirteen years later, after her much publicized affair with Boris Johnson had ended, she looked back on that moment of bliss with Dave, sighing ruefully: "He touched the floor with the grace of Astaire and the manliness of Gene Kelly. Why did I muff my chance to become wife of the next Conservative Party leader?"

Cameron was in Number Eleven on Black Wednesday where the pound fell out of the European Exchange Rate Mechanism at a cost of £3.3 million. In the run-up to the crash, he found himself in a difficult position. When John Major was Mrs Thatcher's Chancellor, he had taken the pound into the ERM. Lamont, though, was not an enthusiast. It was Cameron's job to negotiate the diverging opinions of the two men. He did this with characteristic shrewdness.

"He's not rabidly ideological," said Michael Gove. "He is the kind of poker player who waits and reads the other players and bets when he knows the alignment is in his favour."

Nor did the impending crisis worry him.

"He never has sleepless nights," Gove continued. "He cooks to unwind or watches nature programmes, he is passionate about his vegetable patch and, on holiday, he likes going swimming in freezing cold water."

Indeed as the ERM began to creak, he took a holiday with friends, then one with his family. Then, when he came back, he was seen dining in the three-star Michelin restaurant with old flame Laura Adshead. Indeed, Lamont described Cameron as "a brilliant old Etonian with a taste for the good life".

He was certainly cool in the crisis that would end his boss's political career.

"Just before Black Wednesday he bought me a cigar a foot long and said, 'by the time you have smoked all of this all your troubles will be over'," Lamont recalled. "I have never smoked it."

On the day itself, with David Cameron famously hovering in the background and interest rates rocketing to twelve per cent, Norman Lamont had to announce in the words of his political advisor: "Today has been an extreme difficult and turbulent day. I will be reporting to the Cabinet and discussing the situation with colleagues tomorrow."

That night, Cameron called, telling Lamont cheerily: "There is good news and bad news, Chancellor. The good news is that your picture is on the front page of the *Sun*. The bad news is that it's in the middle of a dartboard."

Lamont acknowledged that Cameron gave him "a lot of invaluable help" over the speech that he had to make at the party conference in Brighton afterwards. Nevertheless, Cameron was in an unenviable position as the tension continued to grow between the Chancellor and the PM. And Lamont had not made things any easier for himself by telling a journalist that his wife had heard him singing in the bath just four days after Black Wednesday.

Matters did not improve when the *Sun* hacked into Lamont's credit card account and discovered that the Chancellor had gone over his credit limit twenty-two times in the previous eight years. "Threshergate" followed. The press reported that Lamont had bought a bottle of cut-price champagne and twenty Raffles cigarettes from a branch of Threshers in a seedy part of Paddington. While Lamont ignored the story, Cameron had to handle the press.

Lending a hand at the Newbury by-election, Lamont lunched with the Camerons at the Old Rectory in Peasemore. Out canvassing afterwards, he was asked by the BBC's John Pienaar: "Chancellor, which do you regret most, seeing green shoots or singing in the bath?"

"*Je ne regrette rien,*" quipped Lamont. Cameron was thought to have been responsible for the Chancellor stealing Edith Piaf's line. It was Lamont's death knell. He was blamed for the loss of the by-election and sacked.

With the fall of Norman Lamont, Cameron was out of a job too. Strings were pulled around Whitehall. Most ministers were reluctant to take him on. However, Michael Howard, who had known him from his days at the Conservative research department, gave Cameron a job in the Home Office, where he became a special advisor to a junior minister. There, it was all hands to the pumps as the Conservatives were in retreat in the face of Shadow Home

Secretary Tony Blair's oft-repeated mantra: "Tough on crime, tough on the causes of crime."

Cameron was also asked to use his influence with Lamont to stop him using his resignation speech to attack John Major, the way Geoffrey Howe had used his to bring down Margaret Thatcher only three years earlier. He failed and Lamont holed Major's government below the waterline, claiming they were "in office, but not in power".

He found himself further out of favour when Howard's name was added to Major's list of "bastards" and Laura Adshead, aka Miss Maastricht, became one of Major's most senior advisors on Europe. So Cameron had to abandon any suspicion of Euro-scepticism and distance himself from his former boss. At the next party conference, Lamont said: "I saw David Cameron, my former special advisor at the Treasury, who cut me dead."

This was not the first time in Cameron's career that he was seen as ruthless.

He got some of the credit for Howard's response to Blair's assault with "prison works". Meanwhile Major was foundering with "back to basics". This invited ridicule. Soon civil servants were jealously complaining that the Home Office had become a PR machine for Howard, who only "talks to young public school gentlemen from the party headquarters".

Cameron was at work behind the scenes too as a member of a dining club run by the deputy editor of the *Sunday Times*, Martin Ivens. It was called the Fellow Travellers and met at the Travellers

Club to discuss the issues of the day. Journalist Anne McElvoy recalled Cameron at a dinner in honour of John Redwood "flushed with excitement, shirt hanging out and waving a large cigar while talking very tough about free markets".

At the time, Cameron was known to be on the hard-right. Introduced to Enoch Powell, he spoke of privatizing the prison service. This was too much for Powell, who considered the penal system the duty of the state.

As well as calling for stiffer sentences, Cameron also wanted to liberalized the licensing laws.

"Licensing has long been a favourite topic of mine," he said. "When at the Home Office as a special adviser in the early 1990s, I wrote endless papers about scrapping our ludicrous laws. The permanent secretary, who was also tiring of my missives about stiff minimum sentences for burglars, summoned me to his office and said: 'Cameron, as far as I can see you want half the population in prison and the other half in the pub.'"

However, when Cameron actually visited a prison, he was shocked and his views became more humane.

Howard found himself in hot water when he tried to sack Derek Lewis, head to the prison service. Cameron was sent to talk to Lewis, though failed to keep a lid on the ensuing row. There was more trouble when Cameron was attacked for leaking the story of a meeting between Major and Labour leader John Smith. However, he managed to help stitch up a deal over so-called 'video nasties' with Tony Blair, meeting the future Prime Minister for the first time.

Despite these ups and downs, Cameron got on candidates' list at Smith Square in 1994. It seemed likely that he would be found a safe seat. Then John Smith died suddenly and Cameron knew his political fortunes had changed. The Conservatives would be facing Tony Blair at the next election.

Chapter Five – Sam Cam

David Cameron's future wife Samantha Sheffield was a school friend of his sister Clare, and was in many ways even more posh that he was. She is the elder daughter of Sir Reginald Sheffield, 8th Baronet, a descendant of Charles II, and Annabel Jones, a businesswoman and socialite who was similarly well-connected. Her family was like something out of a Nancy Mitford novel.

An authentic Tory toff, Sir Reginald was an Old Etonian who can trace his bloodline back to the Knights Templar and the Fifth Crusade, and was president of the Brigg and Goole Conservative Association. Like Cameron's father, he was a member of White's. Other members include Prince Charles and Prince William.

After Samantha's younger sister Emily was born, her parents divorced, though remained friendly. At weekends at the former family seat Normanby Hall, Annabel would book two tables at a nearby restaurant – one for the family; one for the chauffeur. Later, Annabel remarried. Her second husband was William Waldorf Astor III, nephew of her own stepfather Michael Langhorne Astor. For five years, Viscount Astor was a minister in John Major's government and was richer by far than Cameron's multi-millionaire dad.

Samantha said she grew up "near Scunthorpe", referring to the 3,000 acres of arable land in north Lincolnshire that her father inherited, along with Thealby Hall. The main family seat, Normanby

Hall, was leased to Lincolnshire council in lieu of death duties, though the family retained accommodation there. And her father inherited Sutton Park, a £5-million mansion near York with another thousand acres, in 1997. The family had once owned Buckingham House, which was sold off and remodelled as Buckingham Palace, though the Sheffields held on to the furniture.

At the age of eleven, Samantha went to St Helen's, an independent school in Abingdon. In the holidays, she and her sister would help out at her mother's jewellery shop in Knightsbridge.

Samantha first met David when Clare had a party at Peasemore.

"Sam thought, 'Who's this crashing bore who is my friend's older brother?'" said Cameron of his first encounter with his future wife. She was "a sulky sixteen-year-old".

That autumn she moved to Marlborough College, where she took her A levels, and where she dressed as a Goth. Then she took a foundation course at Camberwell College of Arts before going on to study Fine Art at Bristol Polytechnic. There, she tried to shake off her aristocratic upbringing by getting a dolphin tattoo on her ankle, and hanging out with the likes of the musician and actor Adrian Thaws, known as Tricky, who was heavily into drugs.

In 1992, she was invited to holiday with the Camerons in Tuscany. It was then that romance bloomed, even though with her penchant for roll-your-own cigarettes and hippy interest in pop concerts as well as her youth – she was twenty-two to his twenty-seven – she did not fit the obvious profile of a Prime Minister's wife. What's more, he seemed rather serious compared with her bohemian friends, who found the idea that anyone would belong to the Conservative Party faintly ridiculous.

Nevertheless she was soon spending the night at his Notting Hill flat. One of the first stories Elliott and Hanning tell of their courtship is of the phone ringing one Sunday morning and Samantha calling from the bed: "If that's Norman Lamont, tell him to fuck off."

Other weekends, he would drive down to Bristol. Her drug-taking friends were unimpressed. He even got lost trying to find her flat in one of the seedier parts of Bristol and found himself asking directions from a prostitute. The influence of Samantha had the effect of liberalizing him, which immediately brought him into conflict with his boss. At the time Michael Howard was out to ban "raves"; Samantha was a fan.

The relationship was not intellectually challenging. Cameron was a fan of Ian Fleming. Although he had also read Rider Haggard and all of Graham Greene, he generally preferred movies – citing *Lawrence of Arabia* as his favourite, though he had watched *Where Eagles Dare* seventeen times. *Porridge* was his favourite sitcom and his musical taste was mainstream. After a friend took him to the Richard Strauss opera *Die Frau ohne Schatten*, they received a note a few days later, thanking them for "introducing him to Nation Socialism", with the last two words crossed and replaced with "the operas of Richard Strauss".

After visiting the family at Sutton Park, a pair of his underpants, washed and ironed, were returned to him by post with a note from

Samantha's formidable grandmother Nancie, saying: "You left these behind, and not in your room."

From the beginning, Cameron made it clear that he wanted to be an MP. Samantha had no knowledge of politics. She did not know that "One-Nation" Conservatism, originally coined by Benjamin Disraeli, refers to the socially conscious centrist wing of the party.

"I may not have read history at Oxbridge, but I know as much about politics as most people and it means nothing to me," she said.

But while she had no desire to be the wife of a politician, she embraced the role. In the summer of 1993, back in Tuscany, they had to entertain the Lamonts, playing endless games of bridge. Senior journalists were also on the guest list. As a result, Cameron's name was back in the papers.

At the Wyatts' Italian holiday home, Woodrow tried to persuade the women to go skinny-dipping in the pool. Guest Robin Day, the famous broadcaster, was particularly keen. Afterwards Samantha asked who that "dirty old man" had been. When informed, she said she had not recognized him without his bow tie.

In 1994, Samantha and David became secretly engaged. Cameron then told Michael Howard that he wanted to take a job outside politics. Conservative associations mark candidates down if they have not had a job outside politics. Besides, if he was to marry, he needed more money.

Samantha was not so sure about getting hitched. She was still rather young and her mother's first marriage had ended in divorce. But when Cameron sold his flat, she came up with some money and they bought their first home together – again in North Kensington – for £215,000. It was valued at over £1.5 million when he moved into Downing Street.

She also helped him get a well-paid job. He mother Lady Astor had a word with her friend Michael Green, chairman of Carlton Television, who hired Cameron as director of corporate affairs, the only job he has ever held outside politics. Green tried to makes it a proviso that Cameron would not fight the next election. Cameron would not agree to this, taking a lesser position at a lower salary – though still nearly twice what he had been earning at the Home Office.

Sam and Dave's engagement was announced in Nigel Dempster's society column in the *Daily Mail* in October 1994. The engagement was a long one. In March 1996, they had one final holiday as an unmarried couple in the West Indies, returning to make preparations for their nuptials in earnest.

Cameron's stag do involved an afternoon at the races. This was followed by a lavish dinner for thirty guests outdoors in a marquee. There were no strippers.

David and Samantha married on 1 June 1996 at the Church of St. Augustine of Canterbury, East Hendred, Oxfordshire. It rained heavily. One of the wedding photos shows the bride as her customary composed and sunny self, while tears stream down the groom's face. The wedding was a political affair with Michael Howard, Norman Lamont, Michael Green and the Duke of Westminster in attendance. There was little doubt among the guests that, despite her reckless youth, Sam Cam would make the perfect political wife.

By then she had given up her ambition to be a painter. She became an interior designer and professional window dresser, working four days a week as creative director of Smythson, the upmarket stationers in New Bond Street. It was a job again secured through family connections.

As a director of the company she said she earned more than her husband, whose salary when he rose to be Leader of the Opposition was £130,000 a year. But then money was not the issue. At one point, the compiler of the *Sunday Times* Rich List Philip Beresford valued the Tory leader for the first time.

He said: "I put the combined family wealth of David and Samantha Cameron at £30 million plus. Both sides of the family are extremely wealthy. They certainly have no need to worry about poverty or paying school fees."

By then they had three children – Nancy Gwen, born 2004; Arthur Elwen, born 2006 and disabled Ivan, born 2002. He suffered from cerebral palsy, complicated with severe epilepsy, and died in 2009.

In one interview, David Cameron mentioned that his wife "owns a field in Scunthorpe". That may not sound like much, but her father has been heard to say: "I live off unearned income, garnished by the occasional planning consent." In 2007, he was estimated to be worth £20 million.

Now a married man, Cameron buckled down to his day job. He said he admired Michael Green as a "swashbuckling entrepreneur".

He was one of Mrs Thatcher's favourite businessmen. But during his time at Carlton, the company faced a barrage of criticism over the low standards of its shows. Cameron's role was to handle the PR. He was to be the acceptable face of Carlton. It was an impossible task.

Financial journalist Jeff Randall, who has been business editor of virtually every heavyweight newspaper, along with the BBC and Sky, had many dealings with Cameron when he was head of communications at Carlton.

"I wouldn't trust him with my daughter's pocket money," he said. "In my experience, he never gave a straight answer when dissemblance was a plausible alternative. Whether he flat-out lied I won't say, but he went a long way to leave me with the impression that the story was wrong. He put up so much verbal tracker you started to lose your own guidance system."

Randall was not alone in this opinion among business journalists. Chris Blackhurst, City editor of the London *Evening Standard* said Cameron was "aggressive, sharp-tongued, often condescending and patronizing. If anyone had told me then he might become premier I would have told them to seek help."

Patrick Hosking, investment editor of *The Times*, said: "He was obstructive."

Most damning of all is this assessment by veteran City journalist Ian King, who called him "a poisonous, slippery individual," adding: "He was a smarmy bully who regularly threatened journalists. He loved humiliating people, including a colleague at ITV he would abuse publicly as 'Bunter', just because the poor bloke was a few pounds overweight. He was a mouthpiece for that company's charmless chairman, Michael Green, who operated him the way Keith Harris works Orville."

This was, perhaps, not the greatest period of Cameron's life. But then, the tempestuous Green was notoriously difficult to work with. Cameron's immediate boss when he first started at Carlton had been headhunted for the position. She lasted just five weeks, allowing him to step into her shoes.

At Carlton, Cameron maintained his political connections. In 1995, Cameron set up a meeting between Green and the Shadow Chancellor Gordon Brown, telling Green that Brown was "going places". Off duty, Cameron hung out at the Met Bar, a celebrity haunt in Mayfair, or he would go gambling with his boss at the Portland Club. But Cameron was not a natural high roller, playing cautiously even though his losses were guaranteed by Green. They also travelled to the US frequently to make deals. To liven things up with people who did not know them, they would swap identities, with Cameron playing the role of cantankerous tycoon.

Otherwise, his job consisted of giving a "bollocking" to the press on behalf of his boss and lobbying for a change in the Broadcasting Act with his father-in-law, Viscount Astor, then a minister in the Department of National Heritage.

Chapter Six – The Search for a Seat

David Cameron's search for a parliamentary seat began in Ashford, Kent. At a preliminary meeting with the local Conservative Association, Samantha made the mistake of wearing a skirt with a revealing split which had to be safety-pinned at the last moment. Cameron made it to the shortlist. But on the day of the selection, he planned to take the train to the constituency. It was cancelled. Downing Street policy advisor Damien Green arrived on time and was selected.

Then David Cameron came within a whisper of scandal. Money had been stolen from clients' accounts by a young broker at Panmure Gordon, when Ian Cameron was still running the company. The culprit claimed the swindle was part of a botch operation by British intelligence. This had been communicated to the Home Office while David Cameron was working there. Fortunately, neither the involvement of Cameron senior or Cameron junior was mentioned in the court case.

In 1995, John Major confronted his critics, resigned as party leader and called a leadership election in a "back me or sack me" move. Cameron was still in the Westminster loop and told Chris Patten he thought that Michael Portillo should be the next leader. Patten was not convinced.

"He looked at me quizzically and said: 'I am not sure we are ready for a Spanish Prime Minister.' Rich really, for a Europhile," said Cameron.

After missing out on a couple of other seats, Cameron was selected for Stafford, a seat vacated by Euro-sceptic Bill Cash after boundary changes. Cameron rented a farmhouse there and spent weekends in the constituency. Samantha was on hand to put up posters, though in the week she was busy refitting Smythson in an effort to modernize the business.

In 1996, she launched the company's iconic *Fashion Diary*, which carried listings of all the most stylish shops, restaurants and hotels in London, Milan, Paris and New York, as well as the relevant fashion show dates. Its cult status was immediately assured when Meg Mathews bought twenty-two as Christmas presents for her supermodel best friends.

"We were putting gold-stamped initials on them for people like Kate Moss and Naomi Campbell," said Sam, "and the great thing was that they all carried on using them."

The revamped store also became fashionable. Madonna, Harvey Keitel, Catherine Zeta Jones, Liv Tyler, Stella McCartney and Gwyneth Paltrow all became regular customers.

By the time the Camerons returned from their honeymoon in France and Italy, Cameron's political prospects had dimmed. The Conservative government was on its last legs and Tony Blair seemed an unstoppable force. Seeing which way the wind was blowing, Michael Green began employing stalwarts of New Labour.

Cameron spent more time in the constituency, where Cash's majority of 10,900 no longer seemed so safe. As a special advisor to Norman Lamont, he had advocated raising taxes. As a prospective parliamentary candidate attending the party conference in 1996 though, he demanded they be slashed.

In *The Times* that Christmas, Michael Gove indulged in a game of "Fantasy Cabinet". After a period of Blair government, he said, a resurgent Euro-sceptic Tory party would be swept back into power with John Redwood as PM, Giles Brandreth as Minister for Fun and "1997 entrant David Cameron as Chief Secretary to the Treasury, youth would have its head".

It was not to be. With Cameron opposing joining the euro during the election campaign, it was easy to paint him as a Tory right-winger – just the sort the country wanted to see the back of. Nevertheless, family and friends turned up in the constituency to hand out leaflets. The Home Secretary came to endorse the candidate and claim that Labour would put 24p on the price of a pint. But somehow Cameron's campaign never really took off.

Local councillor David Kidney beat him with a 10.7 per cent swing to Labour. Cameron was bitterly disappointed. Sensing which way the vote was going, a lot of supporters deserted him before the returning officer announced the result. Even Sam Cam spent the night drinking the car park with the Monster Raving Loony Party, who had received a creditable 248 votes – though their candidate Aston A.N. May also claimed the large number of spoiled ballots, arguing that anyone who had spoilt their ballot must be a raving loony.

Later Cameron made light of it, saying: "On election night in 1997, when I crashed and burned as the Tory candidate in Stafford, an old lady came to me in tears and said: 'I don't want to die under a Labour government.' Perhaps there were thousands of others like her who didn't wait for the final results and took pre-emptive action."

Cameron returned to Carlton, which was now involved in takeover battles and a disastrous foray into digital broadcasting, ultimately losing out to Rupert Murdoch and Sky. There was a furore when the *Guardian* exposed a documentary on the cocaine trade which Carlton broadcast as a fake. The attack was so dire that Cameron dodged journalists' questions by claiming to the "John Smith". This valiant rear-guard action won him few friends in the press. He tried to bounce back, but even the charm offensive he organized backfired due to the feistiness of Green.

"I've had my fair share of media disasters," Cameron said. "Most of them occur either when you don't know the answer to a question, or when you do but can't say. As well as actually saying: 'I don't know' or 'I can't tell you', we've all tried variants such as 'I'll get back to you' and then leaving the phone off the hook, or roaring with laughter and saying 'who on earth told you that?' But the one thing even the lowliest of spin paramedics is taught is that you must not lie: it means the end of your credibility and it should mean the end of your job."

Some say, at Carlton, Cameron came perilously close to the mark, if not actually stepping over it. If caught out, he apologized. But at the behest of his boss, Cameron often found himself in the position where he had to defend the indefensible.

As the 2001 election approached, Cameron again began looking round for a winnable seat. He tried for Kensington and Chelsea after the death of Alan Clark in 1999, but did not make the shortlist.

In Wealdon in Sussex, he was in the final two, but lost out to ex-MP Charles Hendry who had lived in the constituency since he was eight.

"Cameron should have slaughtered him," insiders told the *Guardian*'s Michael White.

In April 2000 Cameron was selected for Witney in Oxfordshire over Andrew Mitchell, who was accused of sleaze although he had been cleared. It had been a safe Conservative seat but sitting MP Shaun Woodward, who had worked with Cameron on the 1992 election campaign, had defected to Labour. Mitchell was returned for Sutton Coldfield and rose to become Cameron's Chief Whip, before falling from power in "Plebgate".

By this time, in selection meetings, Cameron had learnt to speech fluently without notes, a technique that would stand him in good stead later in his career. This new approach had been Samantha's idea.

The president of the local Conservative Association, Lord Chadlington, offered them a cottage on his estate at Dean, and Cameron went to work right away nursing his constituency.

That December, Cameron turned his fire on his former friend Shaun Woodward, with the letter in the *Daily Telegraph* suggesting that he had made an "unprincipled U-turn" on hunting to sway selection committees in safe Labour seats. Cameron also seized the opportunity to distance himself from "the issue that triggered his resignation – Clause 28 and the promotion of homosexuality in schools". It was a theme Cameron would return to, though in 2013 he backed the bill allowing gay marriage.

On the stump, a local pointed out the pub where the police arrested British Union of Fascist leader Oswald Mosley in 1940, saying: "Apparently Shaun Woodward drinks there now."

"I made some cheap crack about 'the police not bothering to arrest traitors these days' and went on my way," said Cameron.

In 2001, the election was delayed for a month due to an outbreak of foot-and-mouth, so Cameron undertook a sponsored bicycle ride around all eighty-five parishes in the Witney constituency. Covering 220 miles in five days, he raised £4,000 for charity.

"My local Conservative agent is still chuckling," said Cameron. "He applauded my determination, but worries about my naivety: not knowing that 'bike' is slang for prostitute, my press release announcing this caper opened with the quote: 'I haven't been on a bike for years.' Looking back, I can see his point."

Seeing his old headmaster, Eric Anderson, in the street, Cameron ran after him shouting: "Sir, Sir, will you vote for me?"

Cameron took the fight onto enemy territory with a column on the website *Guardian Unlimited* where he called the Labour candidate "one of those I-feel-your-pain, rock-crushing bores" and the Liberal a "human-hamster cross".

Still, he sought inspiration from far and wide.

"There is an iconic figure from the 1970s and 1980s that should inspire the Conservative party this week," he wrote "I am of course referring to the hairy godfather of punk rock who recently died of cancer, Joey Ramone."

Then there was the visit to a medical supplies company in his constituency.

"It markets a new machine called the Rapport, the full description of which is a 'vacuum therapy device for erectile dysfunction'. I will spare you the details (large test tube, small pump, painful looking rubber band)."

He also had some criticism of the electoral strategy of the party leader William Hague, who had focussed the election campaign on Europe and slashing the price of petrol.

"But will these two issues... remain high enough up the agenda to alter how people vote?" asked Cameron. "Knocking on doors in the evening, the answer would probably be no. Education and the NHS predominate, where battle honours are more evenly shared."

It seems he was right. The Conservatives lost the election, though Cameron won his seat and was on his way to parliament.

Chapter Seven – The Greasy Pole

As soon as Cameron arrived in the House of Commons, he had to decide who to back in the leadership election. For a moment, he even considered standing himself, but quickly realized it was too soon.

Nevertheless, a week after being elected, he set out his stall. He told the *Daily Telegraph*: "Millwall fans used to be proud of the fact that 'nobody likes us; we don't care'. The Conservative Party must not fall into the same trap. It has to change its language, change its approach, start with a blank sheet of paper and try to work out why our base of support is not broader. Anyone could have told the Labour Party in the 1980s how to become electable. It had to drop unilateral disarmament, punitive tax rises, wholesale nationalization and unionization. The question for the Conservative Party is far more difficult because there are no obvious areas of policy that need to be dropped. We need a clear, positive, engaging agenda on public services."

Two weeks later, Cameron's name appeared on a list of possible Portillo backers, in the belief that he was going to win.

The parliamentary sketch writers could not wait for Cameron's maiden speech as there was a tradition in the House of praising one's predecessor. He did this with characteristic deftness. Woodward, he said, "remains a constituent, and a most significant local employer, not least in the area of domestic service…" As a Labour candidate,

Woodward had taken stick over the fact that he had a butler, courtesy of his wife, supermarket heiress Camilla Sainsbury.

"We are in fact quite close neighbours," Cameron continued. "On a clear day, from the hill behind my cottage, I can almost see some of the glittering spires of his great house."

His mother watched the speech on the parliamentary channel and phoned up to say: "You need a haircut to stop looking like Peter Mandelson, don't wave your arms around while speaking and tell the man behind you to stop picking his nose."

In the first round of the leadership ballot, Portillo was eliminated.

"The Spanish armada goes down with all hands, including this particular new boy," rued Cameron. "Our man had offered leadership, radical change and ideas that challenged the party both in parliament and the country. They simply weren't ready for it. In many ways it is a view I share."

In the second round, Cameron voted for the winner Iain Duncan Smith over Ken Clarke because, he said: "Mr Clarke's saloon bar habit of calling his opponents 'head bangers' or 'hangers and floggers' always gives me the shivers... Mr Clarke's man-of-the-people, broad-brush approach has minuses as well as pluses. As a former adviser put it to me years ago: 'The trouble with Ken's broad brush is that everyone else gets splattered with paint.'" It was, of course, Kenneth Clarke who had lost him his job at the Treasury when he took over from Norman Lamont.

Cameron was immediately appointed to the prestigious Home Affairs Select Committee, a showcase for new talent. The first thing he suggested was that look into the problems of heroin addiction or changing the law on cannabis.

"On the drugs issue, I am an instinctive liberal (small l, please), disliking state bans on anything," he said, "but my worry has always been the very simple point that legalization will make drugs more available and more people will try them."

Home Secretary David Blunkett responded by downgrading cannabis from being a Class B drug to Class C. Cameron then attacked him for not going far enough. The committee eventually recommended that Ecstasy be downgraded from Class A to Class B and the trial of "shooting galleries" where addicts could inject heroin.

Assessing the new crop of MPs in *The Times*, Michael Gove said: "Media attention, so far, has inevitably concentrated on the biggest body in the firmament – the hulking, shaggy form of Boris Johnson, *Spectator* editor and MP for Henley. Johnson's undoubted writing talent, combined with a hairstyle like a Tongan's skirt and a voice genetically designed to instil fear in Pathan tribesmen, commands attention. But the Commons tends to be suspicious of those who have enjoyed conspicuous success before entering and Boris may have to tread carefully to ensure that his talents flourish. Behind Johnson, however, there are several others who may be the Blairs, Browns or even Mandelsons of their generation. Noticeable so far are David Cameron, the MP for Witney, Mark Field (Cities of London and Westminster), Mark Francois (Rayleigh), Paul Goodman (Wycombe), and George Osborne (Tatton)… Cameron brings all the professionalism and sophistication to politics of one who has worked in both Whitehall and television…."

Following the 9/11 attacks in New York and Washington, David Blunkett introduced the Anti-Terrorism, Crime and Security Bill which had to be debated line-by-line on the floor of the house. Knowing this would attract media attention, both Cameron and Osborne sat in the chamber throughout. They lived near to each other and Osborne would give Cameron a lift home, before they both began cycling.

Cameron was determined to raise his profile. In the *Guardian*, he admitted to being "a media tart. I spent a large portion of the last week negotiating with, preparing for and appearing on radio and television programmes."

He was on Radio Four's *Any Questions*, Channel Four's *Richard and Judy*, with a walk-on part in BBC One's *Crimewatch* in between.

He also confessed: "When a politician turns his back on the mother of parliaments and heads for the studio lights, the green room and the powder puff, the excuses start to flow. 'I need the practice'. 'It is important to use the media to communicate'. And the very self-serving: 'How can I change the world if no one knows who I am?' I fully admit to rehearsing all three."

He had some advice to share when it came to appearing on *Any Questions*: "My tips are: don't drink anything at the dinner with Jonathan Dimbleby before the show; don't worry about the audience in the hall baying for your blood – concentrate on the folks at home.

And try to sound reasonable. Michael Portillo once told me a tip he had been given: by being thoroughly rude and aggressive to the other panellists at the dinner you can wind them up in to fits of indignation. They will then rant and rave on air and you will come over cool as the proverbial cucumber."

His tip for television appearances was to promise the producer a right-wing rant, then say something more reasonable when you are on air, read the schedules beforehand and have some jokes ready.

In the House, as a countryman, Cameron got the bit between his teeth about the hunting ban, heckling Ann Widdecombe and calling Gerald Kaufman a "pompous prat". He took to riding to hounds in his constituency. He also stalked deer and went fly-fishing on Jura where the Astors had a house. There he swam in the sea every day before dinner, whatever the weather, and has been known to take a dip in an icy brook when a guest at other country estates.

He supported Tony Blair over the interventions in both Afghanistan and Iraq.

"I am an instinctive hawk about these things," he said. "Everyone knows that Saddam is a monster."

However, he admitted to being "confused and uncertain" about it. In the end, though, he voted for the invasion of Iraq "grudgingly, unhappily, unenthusiastically". Nevertheless, he gave praise where praise was due.

"Blair himself has been masterful," he said after the vote. "It pains me to say so, but it's true. The speech in the great debate was a parliamentary triumph and it would be churlish to deny it. I've even sent copies to constituents writing to me about the war."

But in the long run he foresaw problems for both parties: "A long, unpopular war ending Blair's reign... Conservatives tainted with support for the government's war."

Iain Duncan Smith's leadership of the Conservative Party did not go well. In November 2002, he sent for Cameron, Osborne and Boris Johnson to help him brush up his performance at PMQs. But while remaining a key advisor, Cameron found he could not support his leader in a key vote on allowing gay and unmarried couples adopt. At the time, Cameron was having problems on his own, spending nights in hospital with Ivan. Though he appeared gaunt and tired to those around him, the *Sunday Times* were soon tipping Cameron as future Tory Prime Minister.

By February 2003, Conservative MPs were petitioning for a vote of no confidence in IDS. Then, after the local elections in May, Crispin Blunt, the Shadow Secretary of State for Trade and Industry resigned, calling Duncan Smith's leadership a "handicap".

Cameron remained in the inner circle and he was made deputy shadow Leader of the House. This gave him his first chance to get to the despatch box. At first, he was thrown by the sledging of the veteran Labour bruiser Dennis Skinner. But then he got into his stride.

Quentin Letts noted in the *Daily Mail*: "This was the best parliamentary debut I have seen."

However, Cameron was nervous of articles saying that he was destined for high office, especially when written by friends. He told a local paper: "It's very flattering but often something like this signals the end of your political career rather than the beginning."

In October, a vote of no confidence was called. In private, Cameron advised Duncan Smith to stand down rather than risk a humiliating defeat. He voted for his leader anyway, but Duncan Smith lost and was replaced by Michael Howard.

Throughout the early years of David Cameron's parliamentary career, he and Samantha had to cope with a severely ill child. He had missed two party conferences to be at Ivan's bedside. In late 2003, he began to talk about it publicly as the Labour government's policy of integrating disabled children into mainstream schools threatened Ivan's day-care centre. What's more, Ivan's condition was deteriorating. He was losing even the capacity to smile.

While admitting it was illogical, Ivan's terrible plight made Cameron more religious.

"Obviously I pray for him," he said. "The truth is the first person who says 'some good will come of this' you want to thump really quite hard, but actually some good does come of even terrible things like that."

Despite the hardship at home, there was still a political battle to fight. On taking office Howard appointed Cameron as deputy chairman of the Conservative Party, then secretly asked him to embarrass the government by preparing a briefing on the Hutton Inquiry that was looking into the circumstances surrounding the death of Dr David Kelly, who had supposedly told BBC journalist Andrew Gilligan that Tony Blair's dossier outlining the causes for invading Iraq had been "sexed up". Somehow the nature of this task was leaked to the papers.

Cameron's report, condemning Blair, was published a few weeks before Lord Hutton's – which unexpectedly exonerated Blair and condemned the BBC. Howard had no choice but to accept Hutton's conclusions before a howling House. Cameron's punishment was to go on *Newsnight*, where he waffled, prompting Jeremy Paxman to ask: "What are you wittering on about?"

Howard tried to make some political capital out of the situation by saying that he would not have voted to go to war if he had known what he knew now, while Cameron reverted to his original position, saying it was right to support the US and the UN, and get rid of Saddam Hussein. A struggle ensued, with Howard abandoning the script that Cameron had prepared for PMQs and demanding that Blair apologize for misleading the country over the weapons of mass destruction Saddam was supposed to have had.

In March 2004, Cameron was appointed "spokesman on local government finance and council tax". Though the local elections were due in June, it seemed he was being sidelined. With the question of Europe top of the agenda, Cameron began holding secret talks with anti-EU campaigners.

The party was growing disillusioned with Howard, and David Davis was tipped to succeed him. But others were already grooming

Cameron. He had even been sounded out to run for the leadership before Duncan Smith had fallen.

In the summer of 2003, Cameron himself began to gather his forces. He persuaded *Times* columnist Michael Gove to stand for parliament. After a period out of politics, his old friend from the Conservative research department Steve Hilton had returned as special advisor to Maurice Saatchi, who Howard had appointed party chairman. He too got himself on the candidates' list.

In the spring of 2004, Gove held the first of a series of dinners in a Mayfair restaurant to start planning what should happen after the 2005 election where defeat seemed likely. Over the following year, these dinners transferred to Cameron's home in Finstock Road, North Kensington. Many of those who attended were from Howard's inner office.

In July 2004, a call went out that "bed-blockers" – Tory MPs in their fifties and sixties holding safe seats – should step aside for young Turks. Veteran MP Derek Conway responded by pointing the finger at Cameron and his cronies.

"This is what we call the Notting Hill Tory set," he said. "They sit around in these curious little bistros in parts of London, drink themselves silly and wish they were doing what the rest of us are getting on with. They'll just have to be a little more patient."

The following day the newspapers carried maps showing where area where the members lived. Hilton told the *Guardian*: "There is no point in pretending. We are mates. We go on holiday and have been doing this for years. We all worked together at Conservative

Central Office in the run up to the 1992 election. That was the origin of the friendship."

One of those named was Rachel Whetstone, who had been at the Conservative research department and was then political secretary to Michael Howard. She was also thought to be Hilton's on-again, off-again lover and the couple were Ivan's godparents.

As interest peaked, Richard Kay wrote in the *Daily Mail*: "There is, I can reveal today, an intriguing romantic spring in the step of Rachel Whetstone, Tory leader Michael Howard's political secretary and queen bee of the so-called Notting Hill set of bright young Conservatives. The Benenden-educated brunette, who is one of Mr Howard's two most senior special advisers, has, I understand, formed a close friendship with a married older man who is a well-connected Tory grandee."

Kay then gave an intriguing hint of who the grandee might be.

"In her role as political adviser, one figure Miss Whetstone has helped promote is David Cameron, 37, the Conservative MP for Witney in Oxfordshire and a happily married father-of-two (with whom she is not involved romantically). Eton-educated Cameron, who is in charge of policy co-ordination for the party, is the stepson-in-law of Viscount Astor, 52, a former government whip and Opposition spokesman in the House of Lords. William Astor lives with his wife Annabel and their three children in a Jacobean manor house in rural Oxfordshire."

Whetstone then confessed she was having an affair with Astor. Cameron was furious for the sake of both his mother-in-law Annabel and his close friend Hilton. The situation was all the more awkward because he was policy co-ordinator and a member of the shadow cabinet. Consequently, he needed regular access to Howard and his advisors.

Cameron was now to take the lead in putting across Tory party policy with articles in the newspapers and an appearance on *Question Time*. He was then put in charge of writing the manifesto for the 2005 election. It seemed to some that Howard was anointing Cameron as his successor. However, colleagues were miffed when, in the run-up to the election, Cameron seemed to distance himself from both the leadership and their policies. Which was just as well. Although the Conservatives gained thirty-three seats, this only put a small dent in the massive Labour majority. Afterwards, Michael Howard decided that, at sixty-three, he was simply too old to fight another election and would stand down.

Chapter Eight – Race for the Leadership

Michael Howard did not want David Davis to succeed him, and Rachel Whetstone persuaded him to delay his resignation long enough for Cameron and Osborne to prepare a challenge. To give him a leg up, Howard offered Cameron the prestigious position of Shadow Chancellor. He refused, not wanting to have to take on Gordon Brown in the House. Instead he became Shadow Education Secretary. George Osborne became Shadow Chancellor instead.

There had been another motive behind Cameron's refusal of the Shadow Chancellorship. He and Osborne had long been dubbed the Blair and Brown of the Conservative Party. But which was which? Being the older, more experienced man, Cameron feared comparison to Brown. Brown had been Shadow Chancellor under John Smith, only to find himself trumped by Blair who had a weaker position as Shadow Home Secretary, not Labour's strong suit. When Cameron heard that Osborne had accepted the position as Shadow Chancellor, he punched the air.

Howard now switched his support to Osborne, thinking he had a better chance to beat David Davis. Meanwhile Cameron was telling the press that he had no ambitions to be leader and still had faith in Howard, though Gove said this was not disingenuous. Cameron was simply "playing his cards close to his chest". However, privately, his parents and, particularly, Samantha were urging him to run. The decision was made in the garden at Dean.

"I remember walking around talking to Sam and thinking right, 'Come on'," he said. "She took the view, look, the Conservative party needs to change, get on and do it."

Osborne decided not to run. As the younger man, he could afford to wait.

"There was no Granita moment," said Cameron – Granita being the name of the Islington restaurant when it was agreed that Blair would run for the leadership of the Labour party after the death of John Smith and Brown would succeed him. However, there were long telephone conversations between Cameron and Osborne before the decision was taken, and Osborne agreed to become Cameron's campaign manager. They both knew that there was one issue that they would have to address in the contest. That was class.

"Am I too posh to push?" Cameron asked in the *Observer*. "In the sort of politics I believe in it shouldn't matter what you've had in the past, it's what you are going to contribute in the future, and I think that should be true of everybody, from all parts of society, all colours and ages and races, and I hope that goes for Old Etonians too."

There had not been an Old Etonian Prime Minister since Sir Alec Douglas-Home in 1964. Home had been a friend of Cameron's grandfather, the 2nd Baronet, William Mount, when they had been at Oxford together.

After turning down the offer to be Kenneth Clarke's running mate, Cameron set about raising money. He had little support among the parliamentary party, but a bid to restrict the vote to MPs was defeated, so Cameron set about creating a buzz in the media and, by the time the competition got underway, the bookmakers were giving odds of five to one on him, making him second favourite behind Davis at evens, while Clarke was at ten to one.

The campaign did not start well, with Cameron making hardly a dent in Davis's lead among the party faithful. His support among MPs barely made it into double figures.

Cameron decided that the best strategy was to pretend that he had already won the leadership contest and was now out to win a general election. His slogan would be "modern compassionate conservatism" and set about buttering up the press. But while the political commentators were wowed, his support in the party was ebbing away. Osborne even accepted an invitation to a house party by Andrew Mitchell who was running David Davis's campaign. There were even calls for Cameron to pull out of the race.

Osborne was not convinced that Cameron could win, believing he was too much of a gentleman to be seen trying too hard. Indeed, when the going got tough, Cameron took a holiday. Even so, when he returned, he refused to do a deal with Davis.

A campaign office was set up in Greycoat Place, just round the corner from Conservative Party headquarters, and an extra £20,000 was raised from backers to launch the campaign on the same day that Davis was launching his. Going head to head with the frontrunner would give him more credibility as a contender.

The venue would be the Whitehall headquarters of the Royal United Services Institute. The journalists covering it had come direct from the Institute of Civil Engineers in Great George Street where Davis had launched his campaign in an oak panelled room.

"The launch was austere. No frills, no food," wrote Ann Treneman in *The Times*. "Dave's launch was just down the road but it seemed to be in another world."

She noted that Cameron had consciously rebranded himself as "Dave" to distinguish himself from David Davis.

"Dave even served us strawberry smoothies. Smoothies at a political launch! Whatever next? Aromatherapy?" Treneman said.

No oak panels here.

"The room was white and circular. The music was calming with lots of little chimes and bells and what-not. I am only surprised that we were not handed little white towels and lavender eye-pads… Even when Dave arrived, seriously late for his own party, the dream-like atmosphere continued. The words 'passionate' and 'caring' washed round us like waves lapping the beach. He kept saying: 'There's a we in politics as much as a me.' It could be his catchphrase because, even in a dream, it makes no sense."

Cameron was improvising. He had decided the day before to abandon the script and speak off the cuff.

Michael Howard had deliberately decided to stay on as leader until after the conference at Blackpool as part of this "stop Davis" strategy. This would give the various candidates the opportunity to parade their talents in a conference speech – something he knew Davis was not very good at.

Cameron was taken to a tailor to have a new suit made that cost over a thousand pounds, while Samantha visited the Marks and Spencers in Blackpool for a new pair of shoes and a selection of ties. Meanwhile Hilton bashed out a daily campaign newsletter that was distributed to delegates. A professional marketing man, he also gave out "I ☐ DC" badges. Davis countered with a big-breasted woman wearing a "It's DD for me" T-shirt.

In his conference speech Cameron again spoke without notes. It was a technique he had now mastered. The speech was a tour de force. It attacked Labour, recalled Margaret Thatcher, promised to "switch on a whole new generation to the Conservative Party" and ended: "If we go for it, if we seize it, if we fight for it with every ounce of passion, vigour and energy from now until the next election, nothing, and no one, can stop us."

There were twenty rounds of applause during the twenty-minute speech and he got a three-minute ovation, admittedly aided by his campaign team who had bagged the front seats. Then the heavily pregnant Samantha came on stage. He patted her on the stomach, giving the photographers a visual image of the new generation.

According to the BBC website, the best joke of the speech was: "It's not just about having a young, vigorous, energetic leader – although come to think of it, it's not such a bad idea." It was not so much of a joke though. Ken Clarke was sixty-five and his speech only got a two-minute ovation.

David Davis's ovation was just one-and-a-half minutes. Malcolm Rifkind said unkindly: "He must be very, very worried because he was speaking to a party of Conservative enthusiasts who wanted to will him to succeed. If he was unable to achieve that, one has to ask the question how would he deal with Gordon Brown over the next four years."

The *Sunday Telegraph* was also disappointed with Davis's performance.

"He should have ripped up his paper speech, stepped in front of the podium and congratulated Mr Cameron on his dazzling debut the day before," it said.

However, Cameron had another storm to weather. At a fringe meeting, journalist Andrew Rawnsley asked him if he had taken drugs at university. Cameron replied: "I had a normal university experience."

"So that's a yes then," said Rawnsley.

The newspapers then demanded that he come clean on drugs, but Cameron adopted the standard defence: "I did all sorts of things before I came into politics which I shouldn't have done. We all did."

The other candidates had no problem denying they had ever taken drugs, but Cameron could not because of his peccadillo at Eton. The *Daily Mail* wanted to know whether his own experiences were the cause of his liberal attitude to drugs.

"Nothing could be further from the truth," he said. "I've seen the dreadful damage that drugs can do."

The first round of voting, just two weeks after the conference, excluded Clarke, with Cameron coming just six votes behind Davis. The next round of voting excluded Liam Fox, putting Cameron ahead of Davis by thirty-three – though there were suspicions in the Fox camp that Cameron had persuaded some supporters to vote for Davis to keep their man out of second place. This was certainly discussed, though Cameron concluded that he could not vote against himself.

These preliminary rounds were among MPs. The two remaining candidates now had to go head-to-head in a ballot of the membership. This was where class became the crucial issue. Fellow MPs knew him for the man he was. But outsiders saw him as a man from a rich and privileged background who surrounded himself with other Old Etonians.

David Davis, on the other hand, was the son of a single mother who had been brought up on a council estate. He had worked as an insurance clerk and joined the Territorial Army's SAS regiment to support himself while he took his A levels. After that, he went to Warwick University, the London Business School and Harvard, before working for Tate & Lyle for seventeen years. This was a meritocratic background Cameron could not match.

But Cameron was a skilful politician who knew how to occupy the enemy's territory. He gave an interview to the *Sun*. In it, he cleverly played down his poshness.

He preferred a pint of real ale bitter or a glass of red wine to sipping champagne, he said, and both he and his wife were Skoda drivers, until thieves burgled his home in Notting Hill and drove off in one packed with their swag.

"The dad of two smokes Marlboro Lights and enjoys nights out at a 'spit and sawdust' tapas bar in the Portobello Road," the *Sun* said. "His favourite telly shows are *Desperate Housewives*, *Lost* and *Spooks*... The Jam and Bob Dylan were his rock idols as a teenager and now he's a fan of David Gray, James Blunt, Radiohead and The Killers. And he relaxes on a Saturday morning listening to Radio Two's Jonathan Ross while chopping logs."

He was an Aston Villa who did not think, just because he went to Eton, he was "born to rule". However, he did want to be Prime Minister, largely for his wife's sake.

"She's fed up with the Tories losing and doesn't want to be married to a Tory MP who loses elections all the time," he said.

How was he going to square up to Tony Blair and Gordon Brown?

"Blair is going to be irrelevant," he replied. "He's soon going to be off on his lecture tour of the USA, stopping only briefly at Cliff Richard's Barbados villa on the way."

While he was brought up in a wealthy family, Cameron insisted that he was not rich.

"I could not afford to send my kids to Eton," he said. What's more he did not own a private jet, or know anyone who did. "I would like my children to go to state schools if they can." Though he saw careful to add the compassionate caveat, "I would never sacrifice my children for my political career."

He admitted he has lived a privileged life but said he understood the struggle of many *Sun* readers to make ends meet.

"I have experienced what it is like, setting out on a very modest salary of £10,000 when I started out in London in 1988 and having to pay the rent on a very tight budget," he said. "I can't pretend I had a tough life. But I don't think many MPs have as much experience as I do of failing public services. I have spent night after night sleeping on the floor of Ivan's hospital room and having a shower wherever you can. It's only when you are on a hospital waiting list and you can't have a test you desperately need for six months that you really understand how painful it can be."

After his experiments with drugs and his time in the Bullingdon Club, were there any more skeletons left in his cupboard, he was asked.

"As far as I am concerned, the *Sun* can put a reporter in my bedroom or around my dining room table and come and see the life that I live and he will see a happy and fulfilled and lovely life," he said.

As the contest hotted up, Cameron and Davis went toe to toe on *Question Time* and Davis got the better of him. A poll then put Davis ahead, with fifty per cent of the Tory Party members to Cameron's thirty-seven per cent. But Liam Fox then endorsed Cameron, evening the field.

There was one final ordeal to endure – another interview with Jeremy Paxman, who had creamed Davis the week before. But Cameron had worked in television and knew that image was all in that medium. So he rang the BBC and insisted that he bring his own lights and make-up artist.

"I did not want to look like David Davis did," he said.

Paxman began by asking if Cameron knew what a "pink pussy" was, deliberately to wrong foot him. Cameron's first thought was that it was a nightclub on Ibiza and took comfort in knowing that he had never been there. Next he was asked about a "slippery nipple". He knew this was a drink. It turned out that these were cocktails sold in jugs in the Tiger Tiger chain of bars owned by Urbium, a company whose board Cameron had only recently resigned from. By implication, Cameron was to blame for under-age binge drinking.

The next topic was tuition fees. But Cameron had prepared a nifty counter-attack.

"This is the trouble with these interviews, Jeremy," Cameron said. "You come in, you sit someone down and you treat them like they are some sort of a cross between a fake and a hypocrite and you give them no time to answer their questions."

Later, when he had been interrupted again, he said: "Jeremy, this is farcical. Why don't we have an agreement? Give me two sentences and then you can interrupt."

Seldom had Paxman been so deftly put in his place.

When the result of the ballot of the membership was announced, Cameron had over twice as many votes as Davis with 134,446 to 64,398.

In his acceptance speech at the Royal Academy, he spoke again of the need to build a "modern compassionate Conservative Party", ending: "If you want me and all of us to be a voice for hope, for optimism and for change, come and join us. In this modern, compassionate Conservative Party, everyone is invited."

Afterwards, David, Samantha and Steve Hilton were driven home in the official car of the Leader of the Opposition.

Chapter Nine – Leader of the Opposition

In his leadership acceptance speech, Cameron was seen to have taken a swing at Thatcherism. Now it was time to meet the lady herself. Told it was going to be a "casual" encounter, Cameron wore a jacket and a crisp, white, open-necked shirt. When he was ushered in, the Baroness, then in her eighties, asked which seat he was hoping to stand for at the next election. When informed of her error, Lady Thatcher expressed disbelief that anyone who did not wear a tie could be leader of the Conservative Party.

Those who had supported his leadership bid were given jobs in his inner office and the shadow cabinet, though opponents were also given a fair shake. David Davis was retained as Shadow Home Secretary and George Osborne as Shadow Chancellor. Liam Fox was made Shadow Defence Secretary, but replaced as Shadow Foreign Secretary by William Hague, who had backed Cameron from the beginning. Hague was asked to restore relations with American Republicans. Ed Llewelyn, who Cameron had known since Eton, became his chief of staff and another Conservative research department alumnus, Catherine Fall, became his secretary.

Boris Johnson, who had entered the House alongside Cameron in 2001 and had backed Cameron for the leadership, was relegated to the position of Shadow Minister for Higher Education. Seen as a dangerous rival, he would remain in that post in a subsequent reshuffle.

Determined not to emulate the split between Blair and Brown, Cameron and Osborne shared a suite of offices in the south block of the Norman Shaw Buildings, formerly New Scotland Yard, and had a meeting at 3.30 every afternoon, along with other members of Tory high command.

"They don't just work together. They eat together and holiday together," Tim Montgomerie of the website ConservativeHome said. "This is a huge operation. Cameron is surrounded by people he has known for years, which inspires loyalty and friendship, over necessarily hiring the very best people. It is a close-knit circle."

In his first House of Commons confrontation with Tony Blair, Cameron delighted his supporters, by saying of the Prime Minister: "He was the future once."

Samantha looked on from the public gallery while the press began calling Cameron the "heir to Blair", a phrase crafted by George Osborne. This was not an unmixed blessing. *Private Eye* announced that this was "the world's first face transplant" and Blair accused Cameron of "political cross-dressing".

Cameron had promised to end the Punch and Judy politics of PMQs and back the government when they were right. His first act was to support Blair's loosening of council control over schools which had prompted a rebellion among Labour's left-wing backbenchers.

"With our support, the Prime Minister knows there is no danger of losing these reforms in a parliamentary vote, so he can afford to be as bold as he wants to be," Cameron said.

In an effort to forge a fresh political identity, Cameron embraced the environment and climate change. He was pictured with a dog-sled in the Arctic Circle and got back on his bike. In the local elections, the Conservatives adopted the slogan "Vote Blue Go Green". But the wheels came off when his official chauffeur, Terry, was pictured driving behind his bicycling boss, carrying his shoes in the car.

Cameron admitted that it was a mistake.

"It happened two or three times," he said. "I now have panniers."

He tried to get local Conservative Associations to select more women and non-white candidates, with little success, and his idea to have an A-list favouring women and ethnic minorities had to be dropped. Nevertheless, the Conservatives moved ahead of Labour in the polls and Cameron used his popularity to demand that candidate shortlists should be at least fifty per cent female. Meanwhile, he identified the issues of the country's "obesity crisis" and Britain's "broken society". Though he denied ever saying "hug a hoodie", the headline stuck.

Seeking to give the party a new sense of direction, he published a mini-manifesto called *Built to Last* ahead of the spring conference. A "beefed up" version was re-launched that August, allowing the opposition to call it *Built to Last a Bit Longer*. The party was invited to vote on it. Less than a quarter did so. While 92.7 per cent of those who voted endorsed the document, compared to 7.3 per cent again, only 26.7 per cent of the 247,394 eligible actually voted in the postal ballot.

Cameron put a brave face on it.

"Today's result confirms that the party has changed," he said. "It shows that Conservatives support the vital changes that we have made over the last nine months... over 60,000 people voted. On anyone's account that is a big exercise in party democracy and an overwhelming vote."

Labour chair Hazel Blears called it a "humiliation" for Cameron. When Tony Blair had undertaken a similar exercise with his policy document *New Labour, New Life*, he had a 61 per cent turnout of Labour's 230,000 constituency party members.

At the party conference in October, Cameron wanted to establish his credentials on the NHS. He told the delegates: "When your family relies on the NHS all the time – day after day, night after night – you really know just how precious it is... For me, it's not a question of saying the NHS is 'safe in my hands'. My family is so often in the hands of the NHS. And I want them to be safe there... We will always support the NHS with the funding it needs."

Class reared its ugly head again in a row about grammar schools, known as "grammargate". This gave the newspapers the opportunity to point out that almost everyone in the shadow cabinet was a public-school boy and Cameron's closest advisors were Old Etonians. This was re-enforced by the publication of Elliott and Hanning's *Cameron: The Rise of the New Conservative* which carried a picture of the members of the Bullingdon Club striking ostentatiously arrogant poses. After that, the use of the photograph has been denied by the copyright holders.

Cameron still had no press secretary. What he needed was an attack dog, the equivalent of Blair's Alastair Campbell. He put feelers out, but among his aristocratic cronies there was no one with tabloid experience. However, George Osborne had already had an encounter with Andy Coulson, when the *News of the World* ran claims from former prostitute Natalie Rowe that Osborne had taken cocaine in his early twenties, before he was an MP. Osborne owed Coulson a favour for deliberately down-playing the scandal in the leader column, a lawyer representing phone-hacking victims said.

In January 2007, Coulson had resigned as editor of the *News of the World* over the first phone-hacking scandal which landed royal correspondent Clive Goodman and private investigator Glenn Mulcaire in jail. In March, Osborne suggested to Cameron that Coulson might be the man for the job. The fact that he was a high school boy from Basildon with no whiff of boarding school was another obvious plus.

At the time, Cameron was planning to give the BBC's Guto Harri the position of press secretary, but Rebekah Brooks, then the editor of the *Sun*, suggested the job should go to Coulson to strengthen links between the Conservative Party and News International. The line was, apparently: "If you find something for Andy we will return the favour."

Once Cameron had satisfied himself that Coulson had not known about the phone hacking, he was taken on.

The Conservatives then launched "Stand Up, Speak Up – The Nation's Despatch Box". It was supposed to have been like Labour's "Big Conversation" in 2003, but more interactive. Cameron asked local associations to organize meetings to discuss policy, while the party's website was to host online discussions moderated by the policy group teams. Unfortunately, with six policy groups in action already, the party had more than enough policy initiatives. The whole thing cost £250,000 and the results were a shambles.

"David Cameron yesterday compared reconstructing the Conservative party to building a house," said a leader in the *Guardian*, "and if the metaphor is correct then he must now be staring at heaps of rubble, cement and copper piping, hoping that the architect's plans come together before the first tenants move in."

The suggestion that the Tories would re-introduce entrance fees at museums and art galleries prompted another row about class, as it seemed to suggest that these facilities should be the preserve of a moneyed elite. It had come from shadow Culture Secretary Hugo Swire, an Old Etonian and early Cameron supporter. He was sacked. In the reshuffle, Cameron brought in Sayeeda Warsi as Shadow Minister of State for Community and Social Action. She had to be elevated to the House of Lords as he could not wait for a Muslim woman to be selected as a candidate in a winnable seat.

On the day, Tony Blair stood down, Cameron praised his "considerable achievements... whether it is peace in Northern

Ireland, whether it is his work in the developing world, which I know will endure".

Blair returned the compliment, thanking Cameron for his "generous sentiments" and saying: "I have always found him both proper, direct and courteous in his dealings with me and I thank him for that. And although of course I cannot wish him well politically, personally I wish both him and his family very well indeed."

Cameron then led his party in a standing ovation. It was clear that Cameron and many in his camp admired Blair for taking a party that had been out of office for eighteen years and making it electable again. By contrast, John Major was a "loser", it was said. However, Blair had already warned Cameron that taking on Gordon Brown the next election would be like "a flyweight versus a heavyweight".

"However much he dances around the ring beforehand he will come in reach of a big clunking fist and, you know what, he'll be out on his feet, carried out of the ring," Blair said, thereby receiving a pat on the back from Gordon Brown.

While he acknowledged that Brown had a "great brain", he said: "We're quite happy Blair's going. He's trying to get out of the shit and can't. Brown thinks he still can, so we have to push his face back in it."

And he borrowed from George Orwell's *1984*, claiming that a Brown government would be " like a boot stamping on a human face – for ever".

With Brown now Prime Minister, Cameron referred to him dismissively as "that strange man in Downing Street". His relations with Brown's right-hand man Ed Balls were even worse. Balls had been a contemporary of Cameron's at Oxford where, unlike Cameron, he had joined the university's Conservative Associations – though, he said, only to keep an eye on the enemy. He also got a first in PPE, ahead of Cameron's.

As Brown moved into Number Ten, Quentin Davies, a Tory MP for twenty years, defected to Labour. In his resignation letter, he told Cameron: "Under your leadership the Conservative Party appears to me to have ceased collectively to believe in anything, or to stand for anything. It has no bedrock. It exists on shifting sands. A sense of mission has been replaced by a PR agenda."

The attack was personal. The letter went on: "Although you have many positive qualities, you have three, superficiality, unreliability and an apparent lack of any clear convictions, which in my view ought to exclude you from the position of national leadership."

Cameron said he was not surprised by Davies's decision to cross the floor.

"Thank you for your support in the past," he said dismissively. "We will watch your future career with interest."

Davies became Minister of State for Defence Equipment and Support under Brown and was made a life peer in the 2010 dissolution honours list.

Worse news came when Cameron's handpicked candidate Tony Lit came third in the Ealing Southall by-election, even though Cameron threw everything into the campaign. He was seen personally to blame.

"Slick communication skills may have been enough to put him on the map a year ago," said the *Sunday Times*, "but the electorate has moved on."

More bad luck followed. Cameron had booked a trip to Rwanda when there was an unexpected flood in his Witney constituency and there was talk of a vote of no confidence. Instead of being seen as the Tony Blair of the Conservative Party, Cameron was now seen as its Neil Kinnock.

But Brown failed to capitalize on his opponent's distress and call a snap election. A couple of shocking murders then allowed Cameron to turn the debate to the issue of crime – traditional Tory stamping ground. Failing to call a snap election made Brown appear a ditherer and slowly Cameron's poll ratings revived.

With Brown's ratings now in the doldrums, it seemed likely that he would cling to power for the full five years. This gave the Tories plenty of time to plan, and now Cameron was getting the better of Brown in PMQs.

Then came the credit crunch which dented Brown's reputation for financial competence, which had been the foundation of the whole New Labour project. Then Boris Johnson beat Ken Livingstone to become London's mayor – showing that the Conservatives were electable. Cameron had not picked Boris for the post, regarding his old chum as a loose cannon. But at the victory party, he held Boris's hand aloft as the winner. Cameron later quipped that Boris would not let go – it was "like the first gay marriage". However, he still had to put up with Boris continually sniping at him from his weekly column in the *Daily Telegraph*.

"I sometimes think there are people in politics who ought to be in journalism and there are people in journalism who should be in politics," said Cameron, "but I'm certainly not going to say who."

There was no doubt in anyone's mind who he met.

The Tories had also done well in the local elections outside London, winning forty per cent of the vote against Labour's twenty-seven. Then the Conservatives won a by-election in Crewe and Nantwich, traditionally a solid Labour seat.

Barack Obama's election in 2008 also augured well for Cameron. Change was in the air. On a visit to Britain, Obama was persuaded to visit Cameron's office – though Cameron had introduced the Republican contender John McCain at the 2006 Conservative Party conference. Cameron could now claim to be a player on the world stage and made a play of foreign photo-calls.

He then tried to woo Rupert Murdoch, visiting him on his yacht and attending his daughter Elisabeth's fortieth birthday party on Corfu with George Osborne. It was hosted by the Rothschilds and Osborne seized the opportunity to visit the superyacht of Oleg Deripaska to solicit a donation. This came out because Peter Mandelson had done the same. However, it reminded the public, once again, that Cameron and Osborne moved in wealthy circles. Tiresomely, class was back on the agenda.

The collapse of Lehman Brothers and the resulting financial turmoil allowed Cameron to attack Brown again on the question of financial competence, drawing attention to the spiralling national debt. Brown and Chancellor Alistair Darling "didn't fix the roof when the sun was shining," he said. They had "left Britain running on empty".

There was a brief respite from the political fray when six-year-old Ivan Cameron died. Gordon Brown was sympathetic. He had lost a prematurely born daughter and his second son had been diagnosed with cystic fibrosis, and he cancelled PMQs as a mark of respect. Every child was "precious and irreplaceable", he said, and that the death of a child "was something that no parent should have to bear".

The country was now plunging into recession. But Britain was chair of the G20 and Brown called a summit in London. Deals brokered there saved the world from financial collapse. But Brown's benefit from this achievement was short-lived when his head of communications Damian McBride was caught smearing senior Tories.

When the MPs expenses row broke in 2009, Cameron came out cleaner than most. Although he claimed the maximum for his mortgage on his constituency home, he only had to pay back £680 he had claimed for clearing wisteria and vines from a chimney, replacing outside lights and resealing his conservatory's roof. He apologized for the excesses of his colleagues and warned that those who did not pay back what they owed would be booted out of the party.

With the economy going from bad to worse, Labour would have to make cuts to balance the books, ushering in an age of austerity. This allowed Cameron to ask: "Who made the poorest poorer? Who left youth unemployment higher? Who made inequality greater? No, not the wicked Tories – you, Labour, did this to our society."

At the beginning of 2010, the year of the election, the Conservatives had a double-digit lead in the polls. They should have been shooting at an open goal, but when the momentum seemed to falter Cameron's vacillation over policy was blamed.

By the eve of the spring party conference, the poll lead had closed to just two points. It was then revealed that Conservative donor and deputy party chairman, multi-millionaire Lord Ashcroft, was a "non-dom", avoiding paying UK tax on his earnings outside Britain. This was just the sort of image the Cameron wanted to leave behind.

Once the election was called on 6 April, Cameron travelled to contested seats in Yorkshire and the West Midlands, reinforcing a classless image by addressing party workers in an open-necked shirt with his sleeves rolled up.

Cameron had long advocated TV debates, knowing that Brown was a poor performer on the box.

"I've been calling for these debates for five years," he said. "I challenged Blair, I challenged Brown, I challenged when I was ahead in the polls, and when I was behind in the polls. I just think they are a good thing."

However, it was Nick Clegg who benefited from the TV exposure in the first round and Cameron, understandably, was less enthusiastic about the next two. With over two weeks and one TV debate to go, Cameron already knew he was in trouble. Close advisors gathered at his house with a copy of the Lib Dem manifesto and their own to begin roughing out a draft coalition agreement. In public, though, they were still warning of the dire consequences of a hung parliament.

On the campaign trail, Cameron made light of the fact that he was being followed by a man dressed as a chicken – a stunt by the Labour-supporting *Daily Mirror* – by pulling off the bird's head. When he was hit by an egg the next day in Cornwall, he got the opportunity to quip, deadpan: "Now I know what came first: it was the chicken not the egg."

With the TV debates at an end, the wind came out of the Lib Dems' sails and Brown made a gaff. Accidentally leaving his radio mike on, he referred to a Rochdale pensioner as a "bigoted woman". Brown had to make a grovelling apology.

Cameron and Osborne spent polling day at Steve Hilton's farmhouse near Dean. Each gave their forecast for the final tally of seats. They knew they had not made it.

Chapter Ten – The Premiership

After the count in Witney, David Cameron was driven back to Conservative HQ, now in Millbank Tower. He was greeted by the party donors who made it clear that he had let them down. Ashcroft had already given an interview blaming the TV debates for robbing the Conservatives of a majority. Cameron knew how ruthless the party could be and faced the very real possibility of being chucked out on his ear.

The object now was to make a coalition with the Lib Dems. The only other possibility was to form a minority government. But this would risk another election within a few months when, Cameron thought, they were unlikely to do any better. By then, the party might even consider running under another leader. However, he could claim some success – he had gained more seats in a single election than Mrs Thatcher ever had and had made the largest gain for his party since 1931. A Con-Dem coalition was the only way ahead. He would brook no opposition.

Gordon Brown appeared on television saying he would remain as Prime Minister while the Conservatives and Liberal Democrats held talks. If their talks came to nothing, he would explore the possibility of a Lib-Lab pact, which would offer "electoral reform" – the proportional representation that the Lib Dems had long sought.

Clearly as the Conservatives had 306 seats – against Labour's 258 and the Lib Dem's 57 – they should take the first turn in trying to form a government. Cameron told the press: "I want to make a big, open and comprehensive offer to the Liberal Democrats. I want us to work together in tackling our country's big and urgent problems – the debt crisis, our deep social problems and our broken political system."

While two teams of top advisors had a series of meetings to thrash out the details, Cameron and Clegg discussed the matter privately. Clegg was insistent on one thing – electoral reform.

Talks had to be broken off on 8 May for a ceremony at the Cenotaph, marking the sixty-fifth anniversary of VE Day. The three party leaders stood shoulder to shoulder in Whitehall. The negotiations resumed the following day.

Clegg and Brown also held talks. There were conflicting accounts of how they went. The Lib Dems were insistent that Gordon Brown would have to stand down as Prime Minister immediately if there was to be a pact. He announced that he would only step down in September after the Labour Party had elected a new leader. Another stumbling block was that even a coalition between Labour and the Liberal Democrats would not give them the 326 seats they needed for an outright majority. Other parties would have to be brought on board.

The Conservatives offered the Lib Dems a referendum on the Alternative Vote, their preferred system of proportional representation. Labour then promised to introduce AV with a referendum afterwards to approve it. Meanwhile, Labour tried to persuade the SNP and other smaller parties to join a rainbow coalition.

When that failed, Brown went to Buckingham Palace to tender his resignation. Cameron became Prime Minister an hour later, though the coalition agreement had not yet been finalized. Arriving at Number Ten with Samantha, he announced his determination to form a coalition government, rather than govern with a minority administration.

At 10pm, Cameron was greeted with cheers by Conservative MPs in the Committee Room of the House of Commons. Shortly after midnight on 12 May – six days after the election – the Lib Dems approved the coalition agreement, which was published later that day. That afternoon, Cameron and his new Deputy Prime Minister Nick Clegg held a press conference in Downing Street's Rose Garden. Their legislative programme was outlined at the State Opening of Parliament on 25 May and Cameron faced his first PMQs as Prime Minister on 2 June.

Asked why he wanted to be Prime Minister, he said: "Because I thought I would be good at it."

Few predicted that the coalition would hang together for the full five years. It has not been an easy ride. George Osborne's austerity policies to cut the deficit were bound to be unpopular with those affected by government cutbacks, pay freezes and benefits cuts.

David Cameron also found himself mired in the phone-hacking scandal. He had brought Andy Coulson with him to Downing Street as director of communications. It was then discovered that he was still being paid by News International after he had been hired by Cameron.

In 2013, he appeared in the dock of the Old Bailey alongside Rebekah Brooks and others, charged with phone hacking offences. He was found guilty on one charge of conspiracy to hack phones.

While the jury was still considering its verdict, Cameron issued a statement saying: "I take full responsibility for employing Andy Coulson. I did so on the basis of undertakings I was given by him about phone hacking and those turned out not to be the case. I always said that if they turned out to be wrong, I would make a full and frank apology and I do that today. I am extremely sorry that I employed him. It was the wrong decision and I am very clear about that."

This drew a rebuke from the judge for commenting on Coulson's guilt before the trial had ended. He was sentenced to eighteen months in prison. He also faced a trial for perjury in Scotland.

Brooks was cleared of all charges, but she was forced to resigned from her position as chief executive of News International after the closure of the *News of the World*. During the scandal it was revealed that she was a close friend of neighbour David Cameron, who used to ride horses on her Oxfordshire farm. They also socialized with Rupert Murdoch's son James. His sister, Elisabeth, is another member of the so-called Chipping Norton set, along with Jeremy Clarkson. Cameron dressed up as The Stig for Clarkson's fiftieth birthday party. It also came out that Coulson had been Brooks' lover.

Under Cameron, British support for rebels in Libya helped bring down Colonel Gaddafi. As the Arab Spring spread, his government sought to support the rebels in Syria after the use of chemical weapons by forces commanded by Bashar al-Assad, but Cameron lost the vote in the House of Commons. This was the first time a British government had been blocked from taking military action by parliament.

"I strongly believe in the need for a tough response to the use of chemical weapons but I also believe in respecting the will of this House of Commons," Cameron said. "It is clear to me that the British parliament, reflecting the views of the British people, does not want to see British military action. I get that and the Government will act accordingly."

Congress followed suit, preventing President Obama from taking any military action. This has allowed the Islamic State to flourish there and left NATO looking impotent in the face to Russian aggression in the Ukraine.

Victory in by the Scottish National Party in the 2011 Scottish general election forced Cameron's government to concede a referendum on independence. As the vote neared, an opinion poll put the "yes" campaign ahead. This caused panic as Cameron feared that he might be remembered as the Prime Minister who oversaw the break-up of the United Kingdom. Gordon Brown rode to the rescue and, with just two days to go, the three main UK parties pledged to devolve extensive new powers to the Scottish parliament if the "no" vote won.

In the end the Scottish people did vote "no".

"I am delighted," said Cameron. "It would have broken my heart to see our United Kingdom come to an end and I know that this sentiment was shared not just by people across our country, but also around the world."

He also faced problems with the European Union, who asked for more than £1.7 billion in budget payments. Cameron refused to pay. George Osborne later claimed victory on the dispute, noting that the UK would not have to pay additional interest on the payments, which would be delayed until after Britain's general election on 7 May 2015.

As that election approached Cameron put strict provisos on the TV debates, fearing they would hurt him again as they had in 2010. He would prefer to fight the election on signs that the economy was reviving.

Clearly, this time, class will not be an issue. While Ed Miliband was the son of immigrant parents, his father went on to have a distinguished academic career. Ed and his brother David attended the same primary school as Boris Johnson in Primrose Hill. Although Ed went to a comprehensive school, like Cameron, he worked as an intern for an MP and family friend, in his case Tony Benn. He, too, read PPE at Oxford. Asked about his "life experience" outside politics, he replied that he had lectured at Harvard and had been a special advisor to Gordon Brown at the Treasury.

Nick Clegg was the son of the chairman of United Trust Bank and was descended from Russian nobility. He was a public school boy, having been to Westminster School, and went on to Cambridge, the University of Minnesota and the College of Europe in Bruges. His wife was the daughter of a Spanish senator. Outside politics, he has been a ski instructor and a journalist. Otherwise, he has worked as a lobbyist and for the European Commission. He is, however, passionate about social mobility. Under the coalition, he set up the Social Mobility Commission under Alan Milburn.

There was, of course, one would-be "man of the people" in the 2015 election – Nigel Farage, the leader of UKIP. His father was a stockbroker. Another public school boy, he went to Dulwich College. He made his money as a commodity broker in the City.

But as Cameron often declares: "It doesn't matter where you come from. It's where you are going that counts."

Certainly, Cameron is going into the history books, which will not judge him on his social class. They will simply have to decide whether he is a class act.

SEE ALSO: *Blond Ambition – The Rise and Rise of Boris Johnson*
by Nigel Cawthorne

Printed in Great Britain
by Amazon

82968354R00066